# TALKING REDS

For Richard and Charlie.
Father and son,
Forest forever

ISBN: 978-1-8380604-1-1


Published by Fulwood End Media. Printed in Great Britain.

INTRODUCTION:



FOREWORD:

# ROLLING IN FROM THE TRENT

'There's something special about Nottingham Forest - you can't quite explain it unless you've experienced it for yourself.'

The words of one of the club's greatest players sum up the aim of this book; to put into words what it means to those lucky few who have pulled on the Garibaldi shirt and worn it with pride.

Sure, lots of clubs can claim a rich history, but few have achieved the worldwide profile of Forest without losing part of their soul.

People who have played for the club talk about the 'family spirit' within its walls, its caring nature for staff and supporters.

Somehow Forest have scaled the highest heights without losing their sense of commonality and community, of teamwork and togetherness. That's not an easy task.

Some of today's biggest-hitters are global businesses first and foremost.

Football clubs in name only, they sell product, not passion.

That's not the Forest way.

Go to a game at the City Ground and the shared experience hits you like a Stuart Pearce snotter.

The stands seep with decades of dread and disappointment, fed-up frustration and fan fury.

But they echo too; to the Trent End's rampaging roar, the passion and pride, the lights, European nights, saints, sinners and last-minute winners.

It's not something you watch, it's something you feel. It makes your day, your week, even your year - or ruins it.

But what about those out there on the pitch?

Do they feel it too? After all, aren't footballers just 'mercenaries', passing through on the way to the next big pay cheque?

Well, read the words on these pages and judge for yourselves.

Having spoken to dozens of past and present players over 35 years as a writer, I can happily report that footballers are among the nicest, friendliest bunch it's been my privilege to talk to.

These ten Forest greats fit that description perfectly.

Again and again, they gave up their free time to retell stories that have probably been heard a thousand times - but never grow old.

'There's something magical about getting it in writing,' one told me, 'It means it will be around forever.'

Let's hope so.

Because getting these words down in old-fashioned print is even more important in a digital age when the world lives in up in the air.

A certain manager liked to keep things on the ground - the ball mainly, but also the feet of his players and supporters.

More than anyone, Brian Clough established what people call 'the Forest way'.

On these pages, you will hear (probably not for the first time) how the great man's moral code was as strong as his philosophy on the field.

Football at its purest, played properly by people who understood the chance they had been given.

To them, the 'Forest way' was the right way, not just to play football, but to live life.

It still is.

So the following chapters, stories, memories and myths aren't just about those who wore the shirt and gave everything on the pitch.

They're about you, me, anyone who holds Forest close to their heart - and all that comes with it; the greatest manager of all time, the legends, the titles, the cups, those two stars, that loving feeling and the mist rolling in from the Trent.

The words on these pages can try to explain it.

But you'll only know what it really means if you've experienced it for yourself.

Enjoy the book.

*Keith Harrison,*

***Author***

# GARY BRAZIL: THE FOREST WAY

It's an interesting thing about the British football public - a lot of people often have Nottingham Forest as their 'second team'. Whether it be national pride from the days when we were winning European titles under Brian Clough or just the way Forest teams have always tried to play football the right way, there's an affinity with the club that goes beyond traditional loyalties.

Older generations will get misty-eyed talking about John Robertson's skills, Trevor Francis' trickery or even a Kenny Burns' tackle.

Others will always remember the brilliant striking partnership of Stan Collymore and Bryan Roy, the rock solid reliability of Steve Chettle and that great team of the mid-1990s; Stuart Pearce, Nigel Clough, Ian Woan and many more.

Younger fans of other teams might wax lyrical about Andy Reid's dribbling, Chris Cohen's energy or Matty Cash's all-round ability.

On top of all this, of course, there's the genius of Brian Clough - a manager like no other and someone who will always be revered for as long as football is played.

Wherever you go in the world, Nottingham Forest is known as one of THE great names in English and European football and all those names have played a part.

I didn't pull on the Forest shirt in my playing days, but I remember coming here and being taken aback by the passion of the crowd - and this was at a time I was playing for Newcastle United, not exactly a quiet bunch of fans themselves.

I also remember looking at the quality of the Forest team and thinking how it was packed with top quality players; Des Walker, Steve Hodge, Lee Chapman and so many others.

As you will read on these pages, understanding the past is a key part of helping young players affect our future. Working in the Academy, we are always very keen to make the youngsters aware of the history and heritage of the club.

There's a responsibility that comes with representing great clubs and learning how to handle that is an important part of the process for the players of tomorrow.

Once that understanding and connection is in placc, I think Forest means more to players and that awareness brings new levels of performance.

Even experienced professionals coming from other teams have found it takes time to adjust to the environment at the City Ground.

It's interesting that Chris Bart Williams says it took him more than a year to fully acclimatise to the new environment when he signed. That speaks volumes, especially as he was a player who had plenty of games under his belt before arriving.

The reality is that Nottingham Forest is a big football club with big expectations and a long-standing reputation for playing good football.

There are cultural, philosophical, technical and tactical areas of the game that we are expected to achieve.

Going back to the Great Man and beyond, we strive to play the game in the right way and conduct ourselves in the right way; don't get involved with referees, play the game correctly and play to win.

Never forget the importance of the badge on the front of your shirt and exactly who it is that you're playing for.

It's funny because sometimes we speak about some of these great names from the past to younger people in the Academy and at first you can see them thinking: 'Who?'

But then they go away and do their homework and you can see their understanding grow.

They go off and watch clips of these great players and not only do their own technical skills improve, but they start to embed and take on what it means to pull on that Garibaldi shirt.

They understand what it is to be part of Nottingham Forest at any level.

The fact that we've got people like Andy Reid and Chris Cohen as part of the Academy staff now helps get that message across too.

You only need to listen to guys like that, or Steve Chettle or Steve Stone - people who gave brilliant service for many, many years on and off the pitch - to understand how special this club is.

I think it will only be when, not if - when - Forest get back in the Premier League, that people will really come to see the size of the place and its potential on the biggest stage again.

The stadium is a proper football arena and everyone knows the strength of the club's support.

The Forest supporters are incredibly loyal and have always been so down the years - that loyalty deserves to be rewarded with Premier League football and I believe it will be soon.

I understand why they care so much - you get drawn in by the club.

It somehow becomes part of you and you're all the better for it.

I've worked over the bridge at Notts County, I had four great years down at Fulham and in my playing days I really enjoyed my time at Newcastle, Sheffield United and Preston North End too, they're all very good clubs.

But there's something special about Nottingham Forest and I'm not just saying that because I've been here so long.

It's like being part of a big family where everyone has the same goal - to get us back into the Premier League where this club belongs, to win things, to add to the club's rich heritage and put more honours on the list.

I hope you enjoy reading about some of the great days the people in this book had with the club; FA Cup Finals, League Cup finals, European campaigns and promotion seasons.

Their passion and pride speaks volumes.

Let's hope we can write another chapter in the Forest history book soon.

*Gary Brazil*

CHAPTER 1

# CHRIS BART-WILLIAMS: BARTMAN

Where to start? Well, I could start at the very beginning and tell you I was born in Sierra Leone, but to be honest, we moved to London when I was only four, so I can't really remember anything about it. *(That's a great start, isn't it?!)*

What I *can* remember is how strong my mum was when we got to England; a single parent with two boys, trying to acclimatise in a very different country - it was hard, but she was amazing.

We learned to appreciate everything we had and saw how much effort had gone in to getting things for us. It was never Nike trainers for us, for example, it was the supermarket's own brand or whatever was cheapest.

But it didn't matter.

It was what we had and I think that upbringing added to the the drive and ambition for me to be successful in whatever profession I took to.

Thankfully, for me, that was football and I know I've been very lucky.

The fashion world probably got off lightly too, as I always wanted to be a clothes designer if I hadn't made it as a player. Come to think of it, *The Bartman Collection* has a certain ring to it!

My style? Well, my teammates would say I've got *no* style, but me, well I think I rock the classic look pretty well for a guy my age. *'Vintage'* sums it up these days, maybe.

I can think of a few of the lads who could have done with my fashion advice down the years. The worst? Probably Viv Anderson - absolutely shocking; like *Lionel Richie meets Lionel Richie's grandad.*

But, hello, I still love the guy all night long.

Luckily I got spotted for my football, not my threads, at quite a young age; I was 11 when I joined Leyton Orient. Not the biggest club, but the right club. And that's all that matters.

Around 13, I had some interest from Spurs, but I just felt comfortable at Orient, even though obviously it was much smaller. There was something about it and I felt I was in a good place to learn my trade from people who knew the game inside out and knew what they were doing.

Don't get me wrong, they didn't make things easy and I probably didn't realise at the time their policy was to develop young players and sell them on - I was just focused on getting that first career step. If that meant I got sold somewhere down the line, well, it was probably good for everyone involved.

As I rose through the junior ranks, I got to see a bit more of the manager there - *yep, the man* - Forest legend Frank Clark.

Growing up, Forest had always been on TV and were a big, big team. I wasn't quite sure where Nottingham was, but I thought it must be an amazing place!

So meeting Frank when I was a kid, he had a great stature, presence and aura about him. But he was also scary - you didn't want to get on the wrong side of one of his looks, let alone hear him shout.

Thankfully, the more you interacted with him, the more you understood him and I think one of Frank's great strengths was spotting almost immediately which buttons to press with which players.

Sometimes it was a strict message that had to come very directly - and I mean directly. One syllable: '*Pass!*' (OK, maybe two syllables in front of that . . !)

Sometimes it was encouragement, sometimes advice, sometimes instructions.

But the best of it was, he wasn't a man of many words. His actions and his decisiveness cut a lot of unnecessary talk out of things. He was very clear, he got to the football point and I liked that.

I was never satisfied with my game at that time and knew I always had to try to do more and do better.

Again, I think that's something that Frank and the coaching staff there liked about me. I was a kid. I didn't know it all, so I was a sponge, trying to take on board EVERYTHING from these guys who had been around football since long before I was even born.

It was a privileged position to be there with them.

I made my debut against Tranmere at the ripe old age of 16, so when people think I've been around for years - yes, I have. But only because I started out so young.

Orient's policy of developing young players to sell worked and aged 17 (and-a-half), I went to Sheffield Wednesday for £275,000.

It was a different world for me, up north - freezing all the time.

Pre-season? Guaranteed sunshine, right? Not in Yorkshire. There's the accent too, *reet*? I'm not saying my part of London was all 'bright lights, big city' (far from it) but it was a bit of a culture shock for sure.

What made it good though was the people were so, so friendly; at the club, in the street, round the city - just lovely people.

Of course, the football kept me busy and my manager was another ex-Forest great - Trevor Francis. I'd gone for quite a big fee for a young man and he was able to help me cope with that, after his own experience at the City Ground, many years earlier.

Trevor was a good motivator and he used that common ground that we had to get the best out of me. Again, he didn't need many words, but he understood a lot of the things I was going through, so that was a real help up there.

In a way, I'm surprised he hasn't gone on to have a more successful managerial career but it's not easy. Playing is hard but managing is even tougher.

One of the key things is understanding each club's philosophy.

As an example, for Trevor, Sheffield Wednesday and Birmingham City are very different beasts - as is Nottingham Forest.

They all have different environments, different cultures and you've got to take that on board, embrace it and then understand where you fit in. I know it took me quite a long time to settle at Forest and looking back, understanding that difference at each club I went to, was a big part of it.

At Wednesday, they had world-class players; Chris Waddle, Des Walker and so on.

Nigel Jemson was there too, but I'm not sure anyone would put him up there with those guys - apart from Nigel himself, of course. *(Just kidding, Jemmo!)*

John Sheridan was a big help to me, again a top player and a very clever player, and someone who would always pass on little tips and advice, talk you through games and things like that.

So again, having someone of that quality alongside you is always a help.

We had some great Cup experiences and I got called up to the national team while I was there, too, so I think it was a good career move that certainly helped my development as a player and a person.

It was also at Wednesday where I met Brian Clough for the first time.

I was coming out of the dressing room quite late at half-time, so I was in a rush to get back out onto the pitch and it's quite a narrow tunnel there.

I didn't want to push past him so I said: 'Excuse me Mr Clough, can I get past?'

He turned round, looked at me . . . and then kicked me in the shin. Just like that. I stood there and thought: '*Wow! Brian Clough's just kicked me in the shin!*'

I didn't know whether to be shocked or honoured to be honest. But before I could say anything, he said: 'There you go son, I might as well give you a kick - because my bloody team won't.'

I don't think I'd have expected anything less from the great man to be honest, but what an introduction.

I'd been at Wednesday for four years before making a £2.5 million move to Nottingham and it was an exciting development in my career for sure. Not for the money, but for the opportunity.

When you go through the gates at Forest, there's such an aura about the place, it's 'deep breath time'.

You go through into the hallways and the reception and you see the honours, the pictures, the memorabilia, the trophy room - it's all so intimidating in one way and challenging in another.

You cannot help but be impressed.

Players are football people and they feel these things. Don't ever think they don't. (In fact, if you don't - get out! You're in the wrong place and probably the wrong career.)

I walked in and I was like: 'Wow. This is Nottingham Forest.'

It was huge for me, absolutely huge. You have to be in a very confident place to be able to absorb all that culture and perform straight away.

And you HAVE to do it. If you don't, like I said, you're probably at the wrong club anyway. You shouldn't be at Forest if you can't appreciate what it is.

But once you've conquered that, understood the expectations, you turn it around and use it as a positive force on the pitch: Yes, this is Nottingham Forest - and I'm part of it now. Take strength from it.

Obviously, when I arrived Brian Clough had not long retired, so he was still around the place at games and things, so that made the expectation to perform even bigger.

After all, I didn't want to meet him in the corridor and get kicked in the shin again!

Irrespective of the fee though, Frank said that I wasn't going to walk into the team and, to be honest, that was a given.

I never expected just to turn up and be picked. Everything you get in life, you have to earn and then you have to try to keep it.

Stan Collymore had just gone to Liverpool but Forest signed Kev Campbell on the same day as me, so I think the club did a good bit of business there.

Not only could Kev play, but he brought a real work ethic with him and a confidence, a belief. You looked up and saw him and thought: 'I'm so glad he's on our side.'

They also brought in Andrea Silenzi and OK, it didn't work out. But, if anything, it was a move that was ahead of its time. The game was evolving, international players were coming in more and more, but we hadn't really done the groundwork in looking after them off the pitch and helping them settle in.

I also think the physicality of the Premier League back then would have been a shock to quite a few players. These days, it is more in line with the top European leagues in terms of contact and challenges, but what sets it apart now is the pace of the game in England.

Back then, it was not only quick, but you were going to get kicked from pillar to post for 90 minutes too.

Also, it was only through my own experiences in the latter part of my career when I played out in Cyprus that I could truly appreciate how hard it had been for Andy to go to a different country and not speak the language.

You walk into the dressing room and say hello, but there are conversations going on that you have no idea what's going on and you can't be part of. The coach comes in and gives his team talk in a foreign language and you have no idea what he's saying. You just nod and hope for the best.

So it must have been really, really hard for him.

There's no way you can be a confident player if you haven't connected with your teammates.

At Forest, a lot of the ball came through the centre midfield area; there were a lot of transitions and it was a key area.

All positions are equally important though and there's a lot of moving parts to make things work, which is why we love the game so much.

That first season I was there, the club was in the UEFA Cup and for me, it was one of the most interesting experiences of my career. People talk about the atmosphere being different on those nights and it's true. As things went on, I think we were the only English club left in Europe and the fans looked on it as if we were representing the entire country - which we were to a degree.

That squad had so much quality about it; Scotty Gemmill was so much more than just a workhorse in midfield, Stoney alongside him could do everything, Bryan Roy was phenomenal - it was just a great thing to be a part of.

The way we played was pure Forest; patient football, neat passing and then hit the opposition on the counter attack. That, for me, was the ethos at the club and I got that.

But it took time - as I said, I'd had to sit on the bench when I first arrived.

It took until Dave Phillips (I think) had got injured for me to get my chance.

And those UEFA games, experiencing different styles and tactics, different pitches, footballing cultures - they were amazing to be part of.

I remember the pitch being awful in Malmo and it being cold - really cold - but then, it was Sweden!

Bryan got a great goal in the second leg and again, the atmosphere at the City Ground that night was electric. I get goose bumps thinking about it even now. The noise when the goal went in - just wow. We had a good team though; a mixture of youth and experience, skill and power and a manager with tactical nous.

The most eye-opening game was Auxerre at their place - because we were BATTERED. Steve Stone scored after about 20 minutes and that was that. We were up against it from then - we couldn't keep the ball, we couldn't get out of our half. We were just hunkered in, blocking shots, throwing bodies at things, doing all the basics and just trying to hang in there and hang on to what we'd got.

But they hammered us really - in both games. So when at the end of the second leg in Nottingham, when we saw their players crying it was understandable to a degree - because they had outplayed us over two legs, but they just couldn't score.

It was old-fashioned resolve that got us over the line and I don't think they could take that in immediately at the end.

Did I feel sorry for them? Maybe a bit. But then again - we'd scored a goal and they hadn't. *Sooo y'know . . !*

Same as against Lyon. We got the goal right at the end of the first leg in Nottingham and then held on out there. Similar to Auxerre, but having come through the previous leg, we were a bit more ready for it.

Then against Bayern Munich, we really thought we had a chance.

To hold them - with all the world-class talent that they had - to a 2-1 in Germany and to come back with an away goal in the bag, we thought it was 'job done' for the first leg. We were happy with that, if I'm honest. It felt like a win.

We knew that we could score goals at home and we were confident.

Don't get me wrong, we didn't think it was going to be easy and we knew we couldn't make mistakes against them, but we were quietly confident.

In the first 25 minutes, we were pounding them but just couldn't get a way through. Yes, they had top world-class players in their team, but we were matching them.

Then, we made one error, the free-kick goes in and after that . . . it went from hard to incredibly hard.

They were 3-1 up with an away goal and the whole context of the tie changed dramatically. If we'd have got that first goal, they'd have had to come at us and we might have picked them off the way they did when we had to chase things.

The margins in the Premier League are small. But in Europe, with away goals, they are absolutely tiny.

One mistake, one goal and everything changes and that's what happened that night. We had no choice other than to go for it, but in doing so, against a top team like that . . . yeah, they picked us off.

Lothar Matthaus came into midfield in that second leg and once they scored, they just turned on the confidence. They knew they had us where they wanted us.

So it was great experience, but also very frustrating. They went on to win it and despite what the scoreline says, we weren't that far away from them.

Extremely frustrating. But that's football.

I thought I was doing OK at Forest, but I was still living in Sheffield and it definitely took me a while to really adapt to playing in Nottingham and understanding everything that came with it.

I don't think the fans saw the best of me for the first 18 months or so.

I think, over time, there was a combination of things that helped. I moved to the city and it was much better not having to drive 45 minutes there and back every day just to get to training.

*One thing I always remember about Forest is the size of the crowds. Even down in the championship, there always seemed to be 20,000 on the games.*

*They were always there for us and yes, there were times when we were awful and they let us know, quite rightly. There were times when they would give us a kick up the backside and that would lift us; shake us out of it, get us going again. They play a part.*

*I did go through spells, especially early on where I took a bit of stick from the crowd and that's tough - don't let anyone tell you it's not. Footballers are human and to hear boos when you're out there and to know they're aimed at YOU . . . that's hard. Especially when you're giving it your all. It's emotionally tough. You've just got to swallow your pride and keep working. Hope that things will turn and they'll see that you are a good player.*

*I've seen people get affected by it and it doesn't do their game any good. It's not like a player hears boos and shrugs it off. It hurts. But the only answer is to keep going, keep working and keep giving it everything you've got.*

*Personally, that's what happened for me at Forest and the fans cracked out the Bartman chant and for most of my time at the City Ground I just played with a big smile on my face because I was loving it so much.*

*Later on, when I left and was playing for Charlton I went over to take a corner against Spurs at White Hart Lane.*

*Just as I was lining it up, this guy popped up in the crowd and shouted: 'Hey Bart Williams - aren't you dead yet?!' To be honest, I shanked the corner - because I couldn't stop laughing so much.*

*I told the lads afterwards and they cracked up too.*

*They said: 'You know what Chris, you HAVE been around forever . . . how old are you?' I was about 32! But having started out so young, I suppose it felt like I was older. Not dead (yet!), just older.*

*In all honesty, I think I got on well with the supporters at Forest and everywhere I played really. They could see that I was giving everything in every game and when I scored and broke out the Bartman moves? Hey, it added a new level of fun! We'd just scored, so I could get away with it. Yes, yes, I know though . . . my dancing sucked! I apologise.*

I was now in and among the Forest fans and that was better for me and it also helped me get to know my teammates a bit more.

I had to get to know the city for myself, work out where I wanted to live and what sort of lifestyle I wanted.

Also, I think I came to terms with what pulling on that shirt meant and learned to handle the expectations a lot better.

Once I did all that, everything kind of fell into place and I really began to feel at home and a big part of things - which is all any footballer wants really. That, and to win things.

But I still say to any player who asks for advice; you've got to get acclimatised to the culture of the club and the city or area that you're playing for. You need to understand the history, the environment, the expectations as soon as possible for you to settle in quickly and start to be successful.

It's the same now as it was back then and that's why players need time to settle.

Find a support unit, be it the club, fellow players, whatever - take action to make the changes to your lifestyle as smooth as possible, for you and your family. Because people often overlook how important that is.

In my first season, we finished ninth, had that good run in Europe and it was probably one of the most enjoyable seasons of my career, certainly being part of the squad with Frank as manager.

I'll be honest, I was looking forward to the second season even more, because I thought we would have gained from the experience and progressed from there.

But as everyone knows, it didn't work out like that - at all.

Where did it all go wrong? Good question! I think partly, there was a hangover where we'd slipped a bit from third the previous year to ninth the following season and expectations had gone up.

We had to surpass what we'd done and that's not easy. Only the top clubs - Man United, Arsenal, Chelsea, etc - have the budgets to keep doing that year in, year out. There was little margin for error at Forest, given where we were on the financial side.

I think we were a well-run club, but United and teams like that, were streets ahead of us in who they could buy.

Players like me - at £2.5 million - had to deliver. The club couldn't afford for you to fail. United didn't have that. They could spend £10 million on someone and if they flopped, they'd spend another £10 million the next year.

So we were trying to punch above our weight at a time when money was becoming more and more important.

Yes, things were bad in that first half of the season. Some of it was down to us and some of it was about what was happening elsewhere in the league with teams leaving us behind.

I don't sit in board meetings, but I do know that losing Frank was crazy. He'd been the LMA Manager of the Year only a couple of seasons ago.

I'm not sure what went on behind the scenes that led to him going, but I think if he'd had the rest of that season, we would probably have done better than we did and may have got out of it.

But even if we were going down . . . let us go down with Frank and he'd be the best guy to bring us straight back up again. He knew the Championship level and everyone was on his side.

There was no 'losing the dressing room' as people outside call it. We were right behind him.

If we'd gone down with him, we wouldn't need to have all the upheaval that a new coach brings, new ways of doing things. We could look at where we'd gone wrong and put it right with some new blood and the same gaffer.

When someone new comes in, it can take two or three years for their ideas and structure to get in place and for everyone to fully understand things. But then what happens? Results take a turn and they're out. And the cycle starts again. It's crazy really.

Even if they'd kept Frank as a director of football or something, there would have been some consistency and it would have been a better way of doing things.

As it was, Stuart took over and did well initially, but it was too much to ask of him.

Dave Bassett came in and obviously everyone had heard of his reputation for being very direct and I was thinking: 'I hope he's not just going to bring that Sheffield United long ball game here - because it won't fit with this club at all.'

I thought the Forest fans wouldn't have stood for it.

But from the first training session, he showed how good a manager he was.

He'd done his homework and he completely immersed himself, adapted his approach and continued the philosophy of Nottingham Forest. He knew the way Forest had historically played and thought: 'OK, but here's some other nuances I'm going to add into the mix.'

Really, the changes only kicked in after the pre-season the following campaign.

I'm not sure much could have been done when he first arrived to help Stuart, but we gave it our all. There was no acceptance of relegation until it was mathematically finalised.

That wasn't in our nature and we gave it everything, we really did.

It hurt like hell for everyone - players and fans - and we were absolutely determined to come straight back up. I know everyone says that, but you could feel it within the squad. There was no messing about.

Dave looked at one or two things, made some positional shifts with players and brought great experience with him. He knew what it was like to go up - and he knew what it took to go up.

There was a clear direction in everything he did. Going straight back up was all that mattered and you either go on board with that or you weren't going to play much of a part at all.

Personally, once I accepted revision, a new way of doing things, it became easy.

I think different managers saw different things in me and I played all over the pitch in my time at Forest.

If I'm honest, I wasn't quick enough to be a wide player or an out-and-out centre forward  (but I did my best) and my favourite positions were probably holding in midfield or pushed up behind a centre forward like Kev Campbell.

Dave played me wide left and I didn't really like the position. But we had a conversation and then I understood it a bit more. After that, it was about developing a strategy to cope with opponents who may well be faster than you.

Of course, I had a young Alan Rogers tanking up and down that side throughout that season, so a lot of it was positional to cover for him when he charged forward and gave us the pace, whereas I concentrated more on passing and holding my position for the team.

Dave was very good at that; looking at areas with problems and coming up with solutions for them. Ultimately, of course, it worked.

He's a very under-rated manager in my opinion and people have a hard and fast idea about him tactically which isn't really accurate.

He was shrewd that season, very aware of what was needed. And on top of that, he knew how to talk to players and get the best out of them.

As for the goal against Reading that got us over the line for promotion, it's a funny story, because it seemed to happen in slow motion.

All of us, professionals and fans, remember our childhood and picking up a ball and catching it just right - it may only be one time, but it sticks in your head! Well, that's what happened with me that day.

We needed the result - you could feel it in the stadium - and Kev Campbell had gone off injured.

Dave Bassett stuck me up front - *y'know, time running out, big game no pressure, thanks boss!* - and I remember seeing the ball from Colin Cooper in the air for what seemed like a long time.

In that moment, the flight and the situation took me right back to a play I'd made in my youth when I was a child at Orient working on my first touch and skills.

Honestly, it was like deja-vu - I can't really explain it more than that.

I just instantly knew what I was going to do. So here we go . . .

*Step one:* I knew my first touch had to be tight.

*Step two:* I felt where the defender was and I knew I had to swivel very quickly because he wasn't expecting me to turn. To control the ball dead in the box puts the defender at a disadvantage, because the ball's not moving and it forces him to make a decision.

*Step three:* While he took a split second to do that, I made the turn - and put it in the net. (Simple, this game, isn't it?)

*Step four:* Celebrate, good times, come on!

It just all worked perfectly and the relief, the emotion, the joy - all wrapped up in one. The fans were going crazy. I was going crazy. My teammates were going crazy. It was, errr, CRAZY.

If you were there, you'll know. If not, get on YouTube and smiiiile.

It was just perfect and ironic too - because we were *awful* that day. Absolutely dire. Not like us at all. It was typical that when we really needed a performance, Reading didn't allow us to show what we could do. They put up a hell of a fight, so credit to them, but we got there in the end.

I remember some of the Forest club staff coming up to me afterwards and thanking me because that goal and that Championship season helped people keep their jobs at the club.

That's how tight it was at the time and that made the satisfaction even more enjoyable, because we cared for the people on the staff.

We knew they relied on us to do our jobs to an extent and there was this great togetherness - the Forest family.

Once we went up, well . . . let's just say it was a testing season back in the top flight.

*

There were multiple reasons why we struggled; a combination of things really that people probably already know about.

Going up, we had some very good players and we had momentum.

Then we lost some very good players - and we lost our momentum.

When you take elements away from a team that's functioning well - and then ask it to perform at a higher level, it is always going to be a hell of a challenge.

At first, I was very confident we'd have enough to do well back up in the Premier League.

But once we sold Kevin Campbell . . . the mood went downhill drastically.

We weren't just losing a big, positive character from the dressing room - we were losing a guaranteed amount of goals.

People may say he wasn't prolific, but he was solid in his performances, in his outlook and his presence. A big, big player has just been allowed to leave. *Why?*

And to compound things . . . we didn't replace him. Again, *why?*

So then we had the Pierre Van Hooijdonk strike situation and suddenly we'd somehow lost BOTH our main strikers going into a Premier League season. Wow.

If you're not scoring goals, it's going to be a tough, tough season. And it was. It's still painful to think about. We'd been on such a high and now we were hitting a serious low.

Personally, I'd have stuck with Dave longer because he's the guy you need when you're in tough situations. He's a fighter.

But that's above my pay grade and when you're a player, you just have to get on with things.

When Dave went and Ron Atkinson came in, the first thing he did was just banish me.

There was no trigger, no flashpoint, I was just . . . out.

I couldn't tell you if he's a good manager or not because he didn't have a lot to do with me and vice versa.

I will never know the reason why, but I was just out of it - completely.

At one point, he told me I couldn't train with the first team or the reserves. I was having Saturday and Sundays off which felt absolutely insane to me. It was completely alien to what I'd been doing for my profession for years.

I remember one training session with the reserves where we were really working hard on fitness and for the first time in my career, it was the one session where I didn't give my everything.

It still stands out to me now, because really, that's just not me.

I was just in a mentally very difficult place. Doing hard running, hard fitness work when you're really disappointed at how you're being treated was tough and that day it just caught up with me.

Eventually the fitness coach shouted across to pick me up on it and tell me to try harder. Looking back, hey, he was just doing his job.

But at the time, I remember just stopping and staring at him - and it must have been a hell of a look!

The reserve team coach ran over and said to the fitness guy: *'Hey . . . today, leave him alone.'*

And that's what I call good management.

It's not that I didn't want to try. It was just that I couldn't process the fact the first team was training on a different field and I was there with young first-year pros.

That felt mean. It felt unnecessary. I'm not saying Ron was callous, but it didn't feel right. How do you prove yourself to a coach that doesn't come to reserve games because he's off doing commentary on the Champions League or whatever?

Especially as the coaching staff that are there are not really seeing what I'm doing and if they are, they aren't passing it on. I didn't feel sorry for myself, don't get me wrong.

But I just couldn't process it, especially when the team was struggling and I wanted to be out there helping.

It wasn't until the Aston Villa game where we had to win to stay up that I came off the bench and got a chance to show what I could do for half an hour or so.

By that time, we were 2-0 down and the die was cast.

To be fair, afterwards Ron spoke to me - and it was probably one of the first proper conversations I'd ever had with him.

He said: 'Why didn't you play like that sooner?'

I was taken aback a bit but I just said: *'I did - but I was in the reserves.'*

He looked a bit puzzled, so I said: 'If your coaches aren't telling you how I'm playing in the reserves, then that's on them.'

I'm not being egotistical, but I was one of the most senior players at the club at that time and one of the people who really understood what Forest was about.

Whether he thought I was a good player or not was up to him, but I thought one thing was for sure around that time - if *I* played well, the team played well.

The club was struggling and I felt the responsibility of being a senior player; I'd been there for several years, I knew what the standards were, I knew what it meant to people, I understood it.

I just wanted the opportunity to play, to help, so it was a real kick in the guts not to get more of a chance under him.

When I did get the chance right at the end of that season, I scored two goals in the last few games and we won all three.

Again he said: 'Chris, I can't believe how well you've been playing.'

It was just bizarre. Why not give me an opportunity sooner? I wasn't an unknown quantity. People knew what I could do. So yes, that was a sad time.

Don't get me wrong - if I'd played, would we have stayed up? OK, maybe not.

But once I got in the team, we had to play through the midfield - the Forest way - and once we started doing that again, results and performances improved. Why we didn't or couldn't do that sooner . . . I don't know.

David Platt came in that summer and he was a progressive coach. Certainly very different from Ron in terms of his approach, especially after his time in Italy.

Speaking of which, I'd always wanted to play abroad and that summer there was interest in me from Sampdoria and Perugia.

But when I went to see the new gaffer he just looked at me and said: 'No. There's no way I can let you go and there's no way you're going. It's as simple as that.'

And you know what? I wasn't even mad at him.

He was building something and I was excited to be part of it, especially after what had gone on in the previous season.

Yes, I still harboured that desire to play abroad, but I understood his position and had no problem with it.

I think David brought with him ideas from his career that were probably ahead of where the Forest squad was at the time.

The concepts were sound, but the players weren't ready for them at that point in time.

It may well have been a different outcome now, as styles have changed a lot over the past 20 years.

I think in his first couple of seasons when we finished mid-table, he was laying a lot of groundwork and these things do take time - to bring in a new playing philosophy that people hadn't really been exposed to before is not a quick thing to do.

I think going into his third year, the mood and confidence in pre-season was exactly the same as when we went up under Dave Bassett.

We were in shape. We understood what was required and there was a real conviction about what we were going to do.

But then . . . he had an opportunity he couldn't turn down with England and it was something new again.

I understand the fans want results fast, but with David, I think we would have got there that season.

*I know some Forest fans may well think differently (!) and I get that, but the bottom line is we will never know.*

What I do know is that when he left, things didn't go well.

The saddest thing about my time at Forest was definitely leaving. It was such a strange time at the club because it all came down to finances.

When we sold Andy Johnson, the writing was on the wall. Because if it wasn't down to finances, why would you sell a player like Andy?

It wouldn't make sense. I spoke to Andy before he left and he was one of the three senior pros at the time with me and Alan Rogers. I thought: *'Oh, OK, here we go . . .'*

Soon afterwards, I got called into the office with Paul Hart and he said to me: 'Are there any clubs interested in buying you?'

I looked at him with a bit of disbelief and said: 'Err, how would I know? I'm not looking at other clubs. I'm happy here and I want to stay. We've got a young team and the makings of a good team. I want to stick around and be a part of it.'

But he said: 'Well, y'know . . . the finances are difficult, you're one of the top earners and we're looking at the budget, etc.'

It was a blow, for sure. I was settled, I was happy at Forest and it wasn't just a money thing for me. The club meant something to me - I'd been there for years and was emotionally attached without a doubt.

But that's football. I was a big boy and I had to take it.

After that, the communication with the club was really through my agent and he warned me: 'Based on the conversations I'm having, this is not going to be pretty.'

Again, I didn't want that. I didn't want there to be bitterness on either side, so I was hoping things could be worked out.

It wasn't a good look for the club to be having these issues with the captain, especially with so many younger players around.

These guys were just starting out and would come to us experienced pros for advice. I remember Andy Reid asking me one time if he should leave and I told him he was crazy - Forest was the one club where young players were going to be given a chance.

People like Reidy, Gareth Williams, Jermaine Jenas - a great crop of young talent. It just needed to be handled properly, guided well and I wanted to help with that.

Not long after, Birmingham came in for me and I spoke to Trevor Francis. I said: 'With all due respect Trevor, it's nothing against you, but I'd rather stay at Forest, as I think we're on the brink of something good here with the team and I want to be part of it.'

Even though I knew they were trying to push me out, I still thought I could contribute and it might change a few minds.

Southampton also came in and again I said no. I wanted to get the team back up and to relive that feeling we'd had under Dave Bassett, to really achieve something again and then if they still wanted me to leave, OK, but I'd go out on a high, having helped the club get back in the Premier League.

So it was a strange one, but there was still hope.

Then one night my agent rang me up and said: 'Chris, you're going to laugh and cry.'

I thought: *'Okaaaay . . .'*

He said: ‘You will not be playing for Nottingham Forest again. They have said you have to leave. It’s cut and dried. It’s over.’

It was a kick in the guts, it really was. I cast my mind back to when I was training with the kids and no-one was even paying any attention to what I was doing and thought: ‘Blimey, this is going to be awful.’

When I put down the phone, I was distraught. This is not the way to end your career at a club where you’ve been for six years.

And to not even get the opportunity for the club to say ‘this is going to be Chris’s final game’ and to see the supporters and thank them . . . that made it even worse.

I can’t say ‘mean’ is the right word - it was cruel.

But that’s what happened. I was stuck in the reserves for about two months doing nothing and trying to keep my motivation up, but in reality, I wasn’t going to play for the club again, no matter what I did.

That hurt.

I was in limbo and eventually the loan move to Charlton came out of the blue really. They were a Premier League team at the time and I was playing in the Championship.

I took a phone call from my agent just as I was about to go for a meal in Nottingham and it all happened very quickly - I didn’t even have my dinner.

I was disappointed that I didn’t get a proper chance to say goodbye to people, players and fans.

It’s not the way you want your career to end at any club, let alone one that’s been a big part of your life for many years.

I remember going back up to Nottingham to collect some stuff and bumping into some Forest fans, who said: ‘Only Forest would sell their captain to a Premier League club while they’re sitting mid-table in the Championship. We’re trying to get to the Premier League, but we’re sending a Premier League player there, instead of taking him with us.’

That kind of summed things up, I think.

The club was saying I wasn’t good enough to play in the Championship, yet they were sending me off to play in the Premier League. It just made no sense. It still doesn’t when I think about it now even. It wasn’t anything to do with my contract in terms of bonuses or clauses for number of games played. There was none of that.

I do understand what the club was trying to do - they were trying to get the wage bill down.

It was a business decision, and I'm sure it wasn't actually personal, but it came across as personal when you're on the other end of it.

How could it not?

I'm not sure who exactly was behind it, it was probably more of a group decision.

I liked Paul Hart, but I genuinely think he was rushing the process of bringing in too many young players too early in their careers.

I'm not saying they weren't good players, but maybe too much was being asked of them at that stage.

Thankfully, we didn't get relegated from the division at that time.

But the way things were being handled, Forest were lucky to avoid that fate.

It's good to have a vision, but we could very easily have been a Crewe; no disrespect, they've got a great reputation for producing young players, but not being able to capitalise on it as a club over a period of time, because there was not enough experience around to grind out results and help in their development.

Because people inevitably grow as their experience builds.

I'll be honest; there were periods - long periods - in my career where I wasn't an easy person to manage. I demanded so much from myself and my teammates and I let that be known.

It was all done with the best of intentions, but it wasn't until later on, as my career developed that I learned the importance of good communication.

I could have communicated a lot better to help my teammates at times, because I really cared for them. I cared for the team and the club so much. Maybe frustration got the better of me at times, but certainly as I matured, I came to understand how to channel those feelings in a positive manner.

You see that with a lot of players. As they get older and go through more experiences, they understand situations better and therefore articulate things in a more productive way. That's how it was for me anyway.

You hear it when you're younger, but there are just some things you have to learn for yourself.

There are lots of things you pick up really easily. If you're a first-year pro and you make a mistake that costs your team a game - trust me, you learn from it. If you don't, it won't matter, because your career is probably not going anywhere anyway.

It's a painful process at times, but it IS a process and once you come to understand that, you actually go looking for things that you can pick up. Then everything accelerates and you get to where you want to be a lot sooner.

That's something that probably applies to clubs too and I just hope and pray that Forest can get back into the Premier League sooner rather than later. It's no good saying 'that's where we belong' - yes, we do, 100 per cent.

But you've got to earn that on the pitch and you've got to learn the lessons that will get you there.

These days, I have my own soccer school out here in Florida and, really, I'm Mr Nobody to most people!

I enjoy being out here and I think there's some real talent just waiting to be discovered and it would be great if some of them could get an opportunity to succeed at Forest at some point in the future.

My job is to develop them and prepare them for that day to give them the best chance of success, wherever that may be.

I teach them a combination of styles really, built from what I learned in England, particularly with Forest but also with Sheffield Wednesday and my other clubs.

I like to encourage them to be creative, but still play within a system. Hey, is this sounding familiar to Forest fans?

I've been trying to get a trip over to the UK organised for some of my young people so they can see the City Ground and see what football means to people in Nottingham.

They've seen clips, but to experience the environment at the club and to see the ground on matchdays, I think they would be shocked by the intensity of it all.

Football is LIFE in England and that passion, that feeling, especially for a club like Forest with all its rich history has to be experienced first hand to start to understand it.

Whenever I go back to Nottingham and drive across the Trent and see the stadium . . . it's still an amazing sight to see and I give thanks that I was able to play there so many times, I really do.

I hope that I never let anyone down, but if ever it didn't go well . . . believe me, it wasn't through lack of trying.

I feel privileged to have played for such a great club and it was an honour to have pulled on that shirt every single time I played.

Even though I've been gone quite a while now, Forest will always be a huge part of my life and I'm just grateful I got the chance to play for them.

I just wish I could go back in a time machine and do it all again - I've still got my Forest shirts, my shorts and I keep my boots polished up.

*I'll even work on some dance moves . . . just in case.*

CHAPTER 2

# IAN WOAN: GENIUS IS SIMPLE

In football, there's a bit of a rule that it's daft to sign someone if you've only watched them on video.

It's a bit like buying a house off the internet without having a look round - you just wouldn't do it. Give any decent agent enough footage and they can make the most average Joe look like a world beater for 30 seconds.

Yet when he signed me, not only had Brian Clough not seen as much as a polaroid, let alone a grainy VHS tape. He'd never set eyes on me.

In fact, I'm not sure he'd have recognised me in a line-up!

I'd come out of Everton at 18 and played a bit on the non-league circuit for about three years in the West Cheshire League, the Welsh League and I ended up signing for Runcorn, while still working as a quantity surveyor.

I was having a really good goalscoring season and by January I'd scored about 15 or 16 goals, so it was going well - in my last game there we won 9-0 at Enfield.

I'd never given up on being a full-time professional, but time flies past and you start to wonder whether it's going to happen: 'Is anyone watching me, no matter how well I do?'

Turns out they were, thank God.

But it wasn't Forest.

Harry Redknapp was on the case and a deal was done for me to go to Bournemouth, who were in the old Second Division back then.

I actually went down there with my dad, met Harry and shook hands on the move but had to come back to work to do my two weeks' notice.

That's the way it was in those days!

On the Wednesday before I was due to finish, I got a call from Barry Whitbread, the Runcorn manager, telling me Forest had been on the phone and they wanted to meet me that night at Northwich Victoria's ground.

I was like: 'Well, I've already shook hands with Bournemouth . . .'

But to think that a club like Forest, who were third in the old First Division, were in for me was mind-blowing really.

I didn't have an agent or anything - no-one did back then - and there was no internet so the story Harry later heard is that Brian Clough saw something about it on Teletext.

He knew Bournemouth had a good reputation for signing decent young players, so nipped in and doubled the £40,000 offer Harry had made. No wonder Barry was keen for me to talk to Forest.

Cloughie didn't come to the meeting in Northwich. It was Ronnie Fenton and Alan Hill - two great guys and that was more than enough for me.

Just to imagine playing for Nottingham Forest was mind-boggling for me, after playing for Runcorn. Don't get me wrong, it was a lovely little club, but to go from non-league to the top of the (tricky) tree was unbelievable really.

Of course, I was then left with the dilemma of how to break the news to Harry Redknapp, so in time-honoured tradition for a young lad . . . I got my dad to call him.

Apparently, there was a big sell-on fee for Runcorn if I left Forest, so they must have been sick of seeing me stay there for so many years after that. Sorry lads.

Obviously, like anyone at any time, I was in awe of Cloughie. He was more than a football manager. He transcended that with his achievements and his personality.

He had his ways but what I always remember is that he was incredibly respectful.

Yes, there was a lot of *'young man'* but also lots of *'please'* and *'thank you'*. He had really firm morals and liked to instil those in young players especially.

He treated me like I was part of the group and I was in with the first team straight away.

To be honest, that was a difficult transition for me, because I walked onto the training ground and saw people like Stuart Pearce there, Des Walker, Nigel Clough - incredible footballers and household names.

I'd been watching these people on telly for years, working in an office on the Friday and then on the Monday morning - I'm in with them at training. *(I think the technical term is 'bricking it'!)*

Roy Keane had just come in and I looked at his intensity and fitness and thought 'wow'.

As a winger, Franz Carr was there and I saw at his pace and thought: 'Blimey - that's the standard round here. I'd better get my skates on!'.

I know you have to get your head round that when you go to any big club, but the jump I'd made from non-league made it a big, big step.

I just had to get on with it and adapt as quickly as I could.

You didn't see Brian Clough at the training ground every day and to be honest, when he did come, you saw his dog Del first, 50 yards ahead of him.

He was a beautiful Golden Retriever and was like an early warning signal. He'd come bounding across the pitches and you were thinking: 'Quick! The gaffer's coming, look lively!'

Everyone would suddenly step it up a gear, people would start doing tasks off the pitch, while others would maybe find hiding places if they wanted to avoid him.

It really was like something off a comedy film.

Archie Gemmill would take most of the training with Liam O'Kane and it was hard but really enjoyable. It may not have fitted in with modern methods and, yes, we played a lot of five-a-sides, but that was the same at lots of clubs back then.

We never really worked on set plays or anything. If there was a corner or a set-piece, you'd know where you should be, but it was sorted out on the pitch and it worked.

The formation was normally a 4-4-2 or maybe a 4-4-1-1. People can turn their nose up at that these days, but when it works well it's a very effective system and that's how we liked to line up.

Everyone knew where everyone would be, you got into a rhythm and you were very familiar with the style of play.

I suppose the only thing was, so was the opposition!

Get it to feet, get it wide, get a cross in, get the full-backs overlapping, get on the end of it and score. That was the plan.

It was a simple format, but it worked.

Things were a lot less tactical in that era and it was a lot more about putting 11 good players on the pitch and giving them responsibility to solve problems and work things out in games.

If the winger's having a tough time with the full-back, go and help him. If their centre half is winning everything in the air, get it into feet instead and see how he likes that.

Mind you, we tried not to put it in the air too often as Cloughie wanted us to play the right way, the Forest way. His way.

I remember one of the things he used to say to me most often was: 'Simple is genius.'

I still use that with young players today.

If everyone goes about their business in the right way, it's a tough, tough thing to overcome. Pass, move, help each other out, keep it simple. If you do that, you don't need to make it difficult for yourselves. People ask what Cloughie's 'secret' was and I think it was that simplicity.

The other thing was, under him I can't remember us ever discussing the opposition.

We never talked about individual players as a group. It was all about what WE were going to do and that's an important mindset.

It makes you feel that the opposition are the ones with the problem from the start - how are THEY going to deal with us?

Obviously, if you'd played against someone before you might be thinking 'he doesn't like it on his left side or whatever' but as a group, the mindset was always about us and the way we were going to play. If things got tough during the game, well, that's when players have to come up with solutions.

That's what you're there for and Cloughie used to say: 'If I didn't think you could do that, I wouldn't have signed you.'

These days, with analysts, tech teams, more coaches, etc, there's a lot more support for players on the field.

Nowadays players want information. They expect it before games. They'll spend hours sometimes studying opponents and shape and things. There's nothing wrong with that at all.

The game's moved on and teams have had to evolve with it.

Back then, it was an individual thing to win your own battle, with the help of your mates all doing the same thing. 'Simple is genius.'

Before games, the gaffer had a tennis ball that he would throw to you in the dressing room. You had to catch it and throw it back.

Sometimes he wouldn't say anything. You'd just catch this ball, throw it back and it was a bit like you were telling him: 'Yep, I'm ready.'

Sometimes he would say something and you hung on every word, but really, he didn't speak that much before games.

There'd be a ball on a towel in the middle of the changing room and he'd get us all to look at it in silence and then he'd say: 'Right. This is your friend. Look after it. All the best.'

And that was it. The bell goes and you're off.

You very rarely got any praise off him - he'd probably say you were lucky to be playing for such a good club and that was that.

Mind you, he did like Stuart Pearce and Des Walker. I'm not saying they got special treatment but . . . well OK, they did. Let's just put it this way, the gaffer never got down on his hands and knees to take MY boots off for me.

Pearcey ran the dressing room and I don't need to tell Forest fans anything about how good he was. As you might expect, not many people argued with his decisions - right down to which music went on in the dressing room.

Obviously, I had him behind me and he kept me on my toes, shall we say, throughout the games.

There was encouragement, abuse, threats, praise, everything - being bawled at you for 90 minutes. It was brilliant.

Especially when I first came into the team, he was great to have so close, talking you through things. But I knew that he was ruthless and if I hadn't done things right or matched the standards required, well, he'd have had me for it.

And I've no complaints about that. You're at a big club and it's not meant to be easy. It's meant to test you. And it did. I loved it.

I was there for nearly a year before I even made my debut, but I felt I was learning all the time.

My dad was an ex-pro who played for Northampton, Crystal Palace and Norwich, who he made his debut for at Carrow Road, aged 20.

Unbelievably, that's where I made my Forest debut, too. It was 10 months after I'd arrived and I was on the bench as we must have had a few injuries around that time.

Normally, my dad would have been there but I hadn't expected to be playing - I'd expected to be helping carry the kit in all honesty.

It was a night game and Cloughie told me on the way to the ground that I was on the bench.

I still didn't think I was going to get on, but the lads were unbelievable that night and were four up with about 20 minutes to go, so I went on for Terry Wilson, I think.

It ended 6-2 to Forest and afterwards, I couldn't wait to tell my dad.

There was no internet, no mobile phones or anything so he wouldn't have known that I'd played.

I didn't even go back to the dressing room - I was scrambling around and eventually found a payphone to ring him up, still stood there in my Forest kit.

Sharing that moment with him was a special, special moment. I was very proud and he was a proud dad - it's something I'll never forget.

Even after that, it took me a while to get a run in the team and it wasn't until the end of that 1990/91 season that I got in regularly.

I remember my first goal well; it was against Chelsea when we beat them 7-0 at the City Ground.

Gary Crosby skinned the defender and rolled it across for me for a tap-in. I couldn't miss to be honest, but it was fantastic to get on the scoresheet for the first time.

I really started to feel like I was getting to grips with things, especially when I scored the winner against Liverpool a few weeks later. Come on - you can imagine how that felt!

I was a boyhood Liverpool fan scoring against Bruce Grobbelaar at the Trent End. It was all unbelievable really, I had to pinch myself at times - and that was one of them.

I managed to score a few goals in the last few games and kept my place for the FA Cup Final against Spurs even though I'd only played about 14 games up to that point.

Having waited so long to get a chance, that was a real confidence booster for me.

You might have heard this before, but it was Stuart Pearce who read the team out on the bus back to the hotel the day before the game.

Pearcey being Pearcey, he was brutal with it: 'Yeah, you're not playing. I knew he didn't like you. You're in. You're out.'

It was just like that - but me? I was in.

I was surprised because Steve Hodge wasn't playing and was only on the bench with Brian Laws as Gary Charles started. Nigel Jemson was left out altogether and I think that was a big call, not to have a striker on the bench.

Obviously, everyone remembers that game for Gazza's tackle and injury and you could see beforehand that he was just so, so hyped up.

He was almost bouncing off the walls, shouting, geeing himself up. You could see he was absolutely pumped up.

We were never really like that. We'd always be calm and try to focus on what we had to do. Pearcey might sometimes say things, but more often he was just all about quiet determination.

That look in his eye said more than any shouting the opposition might do.

When we got out there, well, Gascoigne's tackle on Garry Parker was a red card offence even back then, but he wasn't even booked.

The tackle on Gary Charles after that was just horrendous and really injured or not, the referee Roger Milford, should have sent him off.

Looking back at it now, there's no question about that.

I think it was only the fact he'd hurt himself that kept him on, but that shouldn't have been an issue.

They'd have been down to ten men, we'd still have gone one up and it would have been a different game. Ifs, buts and maybes, I suppose. But it's still painful.

We didn't play particularly well although we got to half-time in front thanks to Mark Crossley's penalty save. But we didn't play as well as we could have. We all know that.

Second half, they equalised and I was taken off, but it just wasn't to be in the end.

I was desperate for us to win because I thought if it went to a replay, I might be dropped and would end up without a medal.

As it was, the goal off Des was an unbelievably cruel way to settle things and we were all just really, really down afterwards.

Cloughie didn't come in and rant and rave after the game. I think he said something along the lines of 'it wasn't to be' but overall it was just very quiet.

It's one of those things that you always wanted to win, especially back then, when it was a huge thing, the FA Cup.

Even now as a group of players, it would be amazing to look back with pride and say we'd won it, because that's what you want to be remembered for - achievements, winning things.

The following year Teddy Sheringham came in and gave us a new dimension up front and I played in fits and starts really, mainly through injury and things.

But I got 20 appearances in and another five goals as we finished eighth again in the last year before this shiny new Premier League thing started.

I think people thought Forest would be a regular fixture in it - we certainly did and maybe that was our downfall.

It was such a strange season where at first it took quite a while for the realisation of the situation to sink in.

When it did, things got disjointed and maybe it was already too late for us. I think one or two people were maybe thinking about what they would do if we got relegated. It wasn't a good situation and it was my first experience of relegation.

Teams had moved on fitness-wise and it was catching us out. There was a new scientific approach taking shape, while we were still doing things the old way.

Sometimes we'd get beat and Brian Clough would say: 'See you on Thursday lads.'

There were lots of reasons, but I think that we were standing still while others were moving ahead.

Unsurprisingly, it's not a season I remember fondly at all, even though I played more games that year than the previous two.

Maybe that's why we went down (!).

To add insult to injury, it was Cloughie's last season. That was the saddest thing, although he wouldn't see it like that I'm sure. He'd say Forest going down was more significant than his departure. And it was.

But either way, after everything he'd achieved in football . . . it was a travesty, it really was.

He deserved better and the Forest fans deserved better that year, there's no question about that.

People may ask whether Brian Clough would have coped in the modern era when there's a dressing room full of millionaires, but I think he would have found a way.

It's hard to separate him from that era, but no matter whenever and wherever football is being played, his words will still make sense: *'Simple is genius.'*

*

Following on from such an iconic figure is an incredibly difficult task; you look at people like David Moyes at Manchester United and others who have followed great managers down the years.

So to bring in Frank Clark was a masterstroke really.

He was Forest through and through, he understood the club and yet he was ready to modernise the approach and bring the club up to date in the Premier League era.

People may say he was under-rated, but within the game he was - and still is - really highly thought-of and hugely respected.

He wasn't afraid to put his own personality on it and put his own spin on everything that Cloughie had set up.

You couldn't just rely on talent any more; you had to be super-fit, you had to do things differently.

He brought in Pete Edwards as a fitness coach and things really stepped up physically.

At first, I wasn't Frank's biggest fan because it was such a big change.

But really, him and Pete saved my career. I maximised what talent I had because I maximised my fitness. Without them, it probably wouldn't have happened.

On a personal level, working under Frank was probably my most successful period. We still had our ups and downs, but he had an 'open door' policy and you could talk to him about things.

He gave me freedom on the pitch and I think those years under him were probably the happiest of my time at Forest.

Getting a goal against Derby from outside the box at the start of that 1993/94 season was a happy time, I can tell you.

We'd drawn the first game at Southend and were 1-0 down I think so to lose to them wouldn't have been a great start but luckily I managed to hit one nicely and get us the draw and things went on from there.

People ask about highlights of that season and really, it's just two words: Stan Collymore.

To work with a striker of that calibre was a one-off really - a bit like Stan. We won games at times that we had no right to win, just because he produced some ridiculous bit of skill to dig out three points for us.

Yes, he's a maverick and a certain type of character off the pitch - you may already know that (!).

But on it, you need that and it was fantastic to have him there. At times, he was unplayable.

I don't think he ever achieved what he should have done when he left Forest. With his ability, he could have gone on to be England's centre forward for years and years and win the lot.

He had a good career, but I'm not sure he ever topped the impact he had on that Forest team.

Dave Phillips was actually Player of the Year that season though and deservedly so. So I wouldn't say the rest of us behind Stan were unsung heroes - it was a real team effort and as a unit everything slotted together perfectly.

We had a really good bond and a centre forward that couldn't stop scoring, so it's a great combination to have - as well as us being super-fit.

Everyone remembers the Peterborough game towards the end and I think that showed our mental strength too. To be 2-0 down and come back to win 3-2 in any fixture is always a great result, but to do in one with so much hanging on it, shows where we were mentally.

The dressing room afterwards was just pure exhilaration (well, and a big dollop of relief mixed in).

We were all just delighted for the club, for the fans and for ourselves that we'd bounced straight back up.

What it gave us going into the next season was a winning mentality, a strong squad and momentum.

We didn't lose any of our key players; Stan was still there and Bryan Roy came in, so we added quality on quality.

Of course, Bryan came in to replace me.

I don't know why, but it seemed like the club was always on the look-out for a left-sided player.

I used to joke with Ian Storey Moore every week: *'Do you ever look for any other positions??'*

Kingsley Black had already come in earlier and when Bryan arrived I was like: 'Really?'

It spurred me on though - a world-class Dutch international coming in straight from Serie A, predominantly in my position? I know you have to rise to a challenge . . . but come on(!).

As it turned out, I had a great relationship with Bryan. He didn't want to play left wing. He wanted to be centre forward and he was brilliant up there too, so that helped me out a bit.

I think initially the club had signed him to play on the left side but luckily for me, it never panned out that way.

It gave me a kick up the backside though; he was such a talent and made the game easy for us with his movement. Every time you got your head up, he was either in space, or on the move into space.

You could just roll it into him or Stan and they had so much ability, we were always in with a chance back in the Premier League.

Once we got the first few games under our belts and got some decent wins, that confidence just carried us through.

Yes, we had a bit of a dip but that winning mentality counted for a lot that season. It was the exact opposite to the last time we'd been up there, when we were losing all the time.

It's hard to explain but wins breed confidence and confidence breeds wins.

We looked after each other on the pitch and we had some great results - I think we were the only team to go to Old Trafford and win that year. (As someone from over Liverpool way, that was, errrrrr, very enjoyable!)

Again we had a goal threat, not just with Stan and Bryan, but if you look at the team - Lars Bohinen bagged, Pearcey got quite a few, Stevie Stone scored and I chipped in too.

So when you've got goals in your team from all over the pitch - including full-back - its a massive help.

Finishing third that season was an incredible achievement, but I'm not being big-headed here - we deserved it.

You finish where you deserve and it wasn't a fluke - we were a very good side.

Our reward was a run in the UEFA Cup at a time when it was still purely a knock-out competition and there were some big - no, *massive* - teams in it.

There was none of this mini-league business, it was all or nothing over two games and that gave it an extra edge. That was your reward for having a good season the year before and it was a proper reward.

That was my most enjoyable season in football, I think.

Even right at the start going to Malmo, where it was freezing, the pitch was cut up, but I enjoyed everything about it - even the travelling.

What we learned very quickly was the importance of the away goals in Europe and that's what got us over the line in that campaign.

Even though we lost 2-1, I managed to score out there after being set up by Bryan and then the return leg we just needed a 1-0 to go through.

Everyone remembers that Bryan got an absolute worldie and the noise that night was just incredible. Obviously, I'd seen clips of Forest in Europe before so to be out there on one of those magical nights was a privilege really - something I'll never forget.

When we went to Auxerre and got a goal early on it was like we'd insulted them in their own backyard: 'How dare you?'

You could see they were a very good side, but we just dug in and put our bodies on the line to get back with the result that night. True grit.

We were clearing them off the line, Mark was making unbelievable saves, it was proper 'backs to the wall' stuff. But you've just got to hang in and hopefully get your rewards.

At the end of it, the final whistle went and we were looking at each other like: 'Blimey! How the hell have we got away with that one?'

They outplayed us out there and it was a similar story back in Nottingham; they were so smooth with the ball. Pass, pass, pass, possession all the time.

But they couldn't score.

They were shell-shocked at the end because they'd played all this beautiful football, but hadn't been able to break down a well-organised, motivated team. We could play a bit too, but there are times you need to hold the line and we did it that night.

In Lyon, it was a similar story. At home, Paul McGregor's goal after Pearcey had a penalty saved had set us up. Over at their place in the tunnel beforehand, for some reason, the skipper was *really* fired up.

He loved the fact we were flying the flag for England in Europe, especially as I think all the other English sides had already been knocked out of the competitions by then.

I remember in the tunnel before the Lyon game we were lining up and it was bitterly cold, absolutely freezing.

It was quite an old stadium back then, so the tunnel was a bit tight.

Pearcey is there, (it's about -10 degrees, so he's got his short-sleeved shirt on) and he turned round, looked at us and shouted (in that voice he has like something out of *Gladiator)*: 'Lads . . . we're not getting beat here tonight . . . because we are effing-BRITISH!'

Suddenly, it didn't feel so cold. It geed us up but I'm not sure what the French thought about it. You could see them looking across and thinking: 'Okaaaay.'

Obviously we got the result after a hell of a battle and, well . . . were you not entertained??

We were on a great run and we were all genuinely proud, not just for the country, but for the club as well. Forest has this massive European heritage and we felt like we were continuing that.

*I think if we hadn't come up against Bayern Munich in the next round, we might well have gone on to win that competition, I really do.*

We were getting better with every layer of experience that the rounds brought and if we'd have got to the final, I think we could have handled anyone.

We were so difficult to break down that even if teams had better players than us, we could frustrate them and hit them on the break. So we feared no-one. As it was, we faced them a couple of rounds too early and I don't care what anyone says, at the end of it they knew they'd been in two tough games.

To go to their place when they had a team of world-class talents - Klinsmann, Matthaus, Strunz, Kahn, Papin - and come away 2-1 was a very good result. With that away goal, it gave us a real chance.

I think when they scored the first out there, they thought it was going to be a walkover.

But Stevie Chettle equalised virtually straight away and you could see them thinking: '*Uh-oh, this isn't going to be as easy as we thought.*'

At the City Ground, under the lights, the first 15-20 minutes we really got at them and the atmosphere was just incredible. It was like a boxing match when one lad is getting on top and just going in again and again. The noise came like waves - just incredible.

We weren't afraid to go toe-to-toe with them that night, but we were dead set on keeping it tight at the back. Our success had been built on not conceding and I think whoever got the first goal was destined to go through. We had two or three good chances but then out of nowhere, we conceded a poor goal from a free-kick that Big Norm will be 'disappointed about' as the commentators say.

You can't really criticise Mark though because he was such a great keeper for Forest and a really top bloke. He'd kept us in it in the earlier rounds. It was just one of those things that set us back.

After that, we had to open up defensively and when that happens against a team of their quality, well, you've got a task on your hands.

Obviously, it ended 5-1 and it looks like a hammering in the record books, but anyone who was there and remembers the game will know that's not the full story.

*

That trip to Malmo may have been cold, but it didn't really prepare us for our fifth round FA Cup tie that year against Spurs at the City Ground. In the afternoon, the weather was fine, bit nippy (!), but no real signs of what was to come. It was live on TV though and come the evening kick-off, everything had turned to white - a proper blizzard.

I'm not sure how long we lasted, but you could barely see your feet, let alone the ball - and somehow Spurs had come out in white shirts.

Eventually the ref called it off and it was one of those where no-one complained.

It turned out to be lucky for me in the end, because in the re-arranged game, Pearcey was still out and I was on free-kick duty.

In the first half, I put one straight through the wall from outside the box before the scored two to go 2-1 up.

Then late on, I think Steve Stone got fouled and the ball was lined up on a bit of a tight angle just outside the box again.

I thought, well, Stuart's not here, I'll have a go . . . and it flew into the top corner for one of my favourite Forest goals.

It was just one of those nights when all the angles seemed to be lined up just right and set us up for a dramatic replay at White Hart Lane that went to penalties.

I scored in the shoot-out but Norm was outstanding - *you may remember his dash down the pitch to celebrate at the end* - I don't think I've ever seen him move so fast! Great scenes.

The only downside was we then went on and got beat at home by Villa in the Quarter Final, when Franny Carr of all people got their winner in a really tight game. Gutted.

In the league that season, we were never in any danger and our eyes were always looking up, not down, so what happened the following year, well, I can't say it came out of nowhere, but it was definitely a surprise.

There were lots of reasons for it, but at the end of the day, you've got to have a front for your team. You've got to have goals and I think that season, we just couldn't put the ball in the net, as a team.

It had been very, very difficult to replace Stan - and I get that; he was one of the best strikers in the country at that time.

And it wasn't just Stan, Lars Bohinen left too. We just didn't replace good players that had left with the same quality.

The club made some good signings - Kev Campbell and Chris Bart Williams were great.

Chris was a real talent in my opinion. He could do everything, left foot, right foot and he could have done more really. He was a laid back kid, but a really good player, probably under-rated during his career for his ability.

But overall, that spark up front was missing and it cost us. Bryan was in and out after one or two injuries and we never really got going.

I got a goal against Liverpool at Anfield, and I think I might have finished joint top scorer in the league with eight goals, which tells its own story really.

You need a striker that's getting you a minimum 15 goals and that gives the entire team a lift.

No disrespect to the lads that we had, but we didn't have those goals in us. Without that, the pressure that goes on your back four is huge because you know if you concede one, you're going to be struggling for a win at that level.

You can't just defend your way through a season.

It's obviously not a year that anyone remembers fondly at all. Painful, really painful, as we were down at the wrong end of the table almost all the way through.

Obviously, Frank went and I don't think that helped matters. Stuart took over for a while, but it was a tough ask for his first time as player/manager, then Dave Bassett came in to help and everything was a bit up in the air.

Pierre van Hooijdonk arrived, but it was all a bit late in the day.

To be rock bottom was painful, but you finish where you deserve and that was us - 20th.

It was up to us to bounce back again, but there was a frustration about us lads who'd been there for a while that we were back in that situation. It just added to our determination to get back up ASAP.

We just had to make sure we put things right again and the following year was even better than the last time we'd been down there as we came back as Champions.

Obviously, Pearcey left and Dave took over full-time and did a great job that year.

As a manager, I think he got tarred with the Wimbledon brush about being direct, but that's disrespectful when you look at the success he had elsewhere too, including Forest.

I don't think we suddenly became a long-ball team, there was a lot of football played.

Dave was a really good manager, really enthusiastic and he knew the game inside out.

He was a good coach in training, very clear about what he wanted, how to go about things and it paid off. I really enjoyed working with him, even though I maybe wasn't his type of player.

He wanted a more robust team and I think he probably saw me as one of the old guard, but that wasn't the real problem I had that season.

I had a real issue with chronic tendonitis in my right knee - the leg I really only used for standing on.

But it just kept deteriorating and getting worse. I'd have injections but it massively limited what I could do. I could barely even get through training and it had a huge effect on my performances.

I didn't want to come out and use the injury as an excuse, but I was trying to manage it and get through but I knew I wasn't able to do what I'd been doing before.

I'd play in some games, but I'm not sure I lasted 90 minutes in many so I often had to watch from the sidelines that season.

Thankfully, Pierre was just outstanding for us, he could score goals from anywhere and his set pieces were unbelievable.

He was one of the best I've ever seen for free-kicks outside the box. What a player and what a season that was.

Again, we just clicked at the lower level and were rolling teams over at times as we had goals back in the side; Kev Campbell was great foil for Pierre and did so much work setting things up.

Colin Cooper and Chetts were solid at the back and we still had quality in midfield, so again it was a mixture of joy and relief when we came straight back up. You just hoped we'd learned the lessons from the past.

As it turned out, I'm not sure we had.

The club sold Kev and then Pierre did what Pierre did.

Look, he had a point, but he went about it in totally the wrong way.

His argument was that we were going into the Premier League with a weaker side than we'd been promoted with.

You want to be looking down the tunnel before a game and be thinking: 'Yes, these lads will do for me today.'

So I think people agreed with what he was saying - we'd had the heart ripped out of the team a bit.

But he should have come and got in the trenches with us at least.

At least fight. Don't just stop and leave us to it.

Instead he had the mentality that he wasn't happy with what the club was doing and he wanted out.

But clearly he didn't go about it the right way.

The whole thing just disrailed us a bit going into that season when we should have been really positive about being back in the Premier League.

We didn't look like we had a plan and we were always reacting to things, so again it was tough to see.

Personally, I'd reached a big decision that summer anyway - the knee injury needed an operation. I just wasn't able to train or perform properly any more without it and so I didn't kick a ball after that for more than 12 months.

In all honesty, I should have had the operation sooner. I'd scrambled through the season before when I should really just have bitten the bullet and got it done.

After the operation . . . I was never the same player, to be honest.

I had glimpses but never on a consistent basis. I think five players from around and about had the same surgery that summer and I was the only one who made it back in any real capacity.

By the time I got back, Dave Bassett had gone, Ron Atkinson had been and gone and David Platt was now in charge.

My last year was a sad one because I didn't really see eye-to-eye with David.

He didn't treat me all that well and it was clear he wanted me out, so I didn't have a good relationship with him. We just clashed, really.

Forest has got an incredible 'family feeling' and he was starting to rip that out in my opinion.

There was an arrogance with him and he didn't want to be associated with the past.

For me, you've got to remember the past and build on it, not be disrespectful.

You've got the two stars on your shirt; you've got to embrace that and feel massive pride in it.

The John Robertson, Peter Shilton, Trevor Francis, Tony Woodcock era and everything they achieved is part of the heritage of this brilliant club. Don't try and diminish it.

I'm not bitter now, but it left a bit of a sour taste at the time if I'm honest.

I was getting odd appearances off the bench and my last game was 12 minutes or so away at Stockport in the Championship.

There were Forest fans everywhere, but the football was poor and it was just miles off where we should have been for the club. *Miles away.*

I remember coming off the bus, getting in my car, driving out of the gates for the last time and thinking: *'Blimey, is that it? Am I done? Is this the end here?'*

It was just such a sad feeling. I got home and I was sat there thinking: 'That was my last game. It's over.'

I couldn't get my head round it at first, I really couldn't.

I think one of my biggest frustrations was not being able to say goodbye to the fans properly. I didn't expect a parade or anything (!), but it would have nice just to be able to thank everyone at the club for their support over the years.

It took a while to sink in, because Forest had been such a huge part of my life - and it still is.

After the team that's paying my wages, it's always the result I look out for first. It still feels like my club. It always will be.

It's where most people remember me as a player and where I had so many good times.

I look back over that 1990s period and you could rattle off 20 players who were top, top class to grace the Forest shirt over that time.

It was a wonderful thing to be a part of and a great time to be there.

I know we bounced up and down a couple of times, but we always had a talented team.

We always tried to play the right way. People talk about 'the Forest way' and it's still a thing - it's a club that for as long as you remember has always set out to play good football.

These days, I look back on my playing career at the City Ground and think how lucky I was to have been there.

To have played for Brian Clough, to have played in some great games, scored a few goals that people remember, just to have pulled on the shirt . . . it all makes me very proud.

*I'm not just saying this but it's a special place and I just feel privileged to have played a small part in its wonderful history.*

CHAPTER 3

# DAVID PHILLIPS: AWAY TOO LONG

Everyone knows football is a short career - especially footballers. One minute you're cleaning boots and the next you're hanging them up for good.

The bit in the middle goes by in a flash and you've just got to cram in as much as possible.

People *(well, clubs and the media mainly)* often talk about players being the *'wrong side of 30'* and when you hit that landmark . . . you know the clock is really ticking then.

Some fellas drift into it and accept their time is coming to an end.

No thanks. That's not me. I joined Nottingham Forest and had one of the best spells of my career.

My move to the City Ground actually stemmed from a contract offer I'd had at Norwich.

We'd just finished third in the Premier League and, though I say it myself, I'd had an excellent season, with the club qualifying to play in the UEFA Cup. We'd done really well as a team.

So everything was going good but then the contract they offered me was, well, disparaging, to be honest. I couldn't get my head round it and still can't to be honest.

But out of a negative came a great positive in my career.

Through the PFA, I had an enquiry come in from Frank Clark and obviously, the thought of playing for Nottingham Forest was a big attraction.

Norwich went off to America on pre-season but I stayed behind, training with the kids, while things were sorted out.

In the end, it went to a tribunal in London and I think the fee was £550,000, which I think was somewhere in the middle between what the two clubs were offering.

I was at the dreaded 30 by then so it was a decent fee for someone on the *'wrong side'* of that age but I was still hungry for success.

I wasn't looking for a last payday or an easy way out at a lower level - I was determined to achieve something with Forest.

I'd had four good years at Carrow Road and done well in the Premier League, whereas Forest had just been relegated and were looking at a season at least in the old (or should that be new?) First Division.

But that never bothered me. I looked at the size of the club, the history, the fanbase and it was an easy decision to make.

I also thought that Forest under Frank would have an excellent chance of coming straight back up - and happily that's how it turned out.

Roy Keane had just left for Manchester United and I think Frank saw me as someone who could fill in that pivotal midfield role to replace a bit of what Roy had brought to the team.

We weren't exactly the same type of player (!), but there were similarities in us in that central midfield area in terms of positional nous and being able to launch attacks.

Frank was a lovable guy and I've still got so much respect for him even now - I can't say that about every manager I've played under, so when you find someone like that, you really want to make the most of it.

And that's what we did.

He was always very straight down the line with you, very true in what he said and what he did.

Again, that's not something you find everywhere in football.

I think his presence persuaded the likes of Stuart Pearce to stay with the club when Forest went down and I'm not sure other managers would have been able to do that.

But when I looked round the dressing room at the squad, I thought: 'What are these players doing at this level?'

Stuart, an England international, Steve Chettle, Colin Cooper, Mark Crossley, Steve Stone, Scot Gemmill, Ian Woan . . . all players with top flight experience who should have been in the Premier League.

I didn't know exactly what had gone wrong the season before, but for me, it was a case of looking forward and I thought surely we had a great chance of going straight back up with those guys.

I'd played for Plymouth, Manchester City and Coventry before Norwich so I'd moved around a bit but always to good clubs and I thought Forest were in exactly that same mould.

When I was growing up, my dad was in the RAF so I'd got used to moving around a bit.

I'd spent time in the Midlands before and it gave me a chance to move back there, where I liked it and felt at home.

I became great friends with Kingsley Black and we ended up having a flat together in Bridgford, where we'd stay in the week. It was only a ten-minute walk to training if we fancied a stroll (I'll be honest - we normally drove!) and it was great to be among the people you were representing on a Saturday afternoon.

Kingsley was from Luton and he's a great guy, as well as a fantastic player, while home for me was Leamington Spa, so the flat worked well. We were both fairly tidy, so it wasn't Men Behaving Badly or anything like that.

These days obviously, teams prepare for home games by staying in hotels, but for us we'd just prepare in the flat, talking about opposition players sometimes and focusing on the game ahead.

Away games, we always stayed away the night before, even if we were only playing in Derby.

We did stay somewhere before a home game once and ended up turning up late at the City Ground after getting caught in traffic. It turned into a bit of a team-building exercise, with all sorts of jokes and banter flying about, although I'm not sure what the driver made of it. It's always easier to have a laugh when you're not the ones at fault (!).

Frank did modernise things, but in all honesty, he didn't do a great deal of the actual training sessions.

Liam O'Kane did most of that and there was Pete Edwards, a great sports scientist, who really built up the overall fitness.

There's a lot of talk about the five-a-sides in previous eras, but there's a lot to be said for them in all honesty. We still did quite a few and you can take a lot from those games; they're quick, they test you and they keep you sharp.

I think Frank built on things rather than just throw everything out with the bathwater.

He'd work a lot on different patterns of play, different phases, transitions as they call them now, between being in possession and being without the ball.

That positional play was very much a part of our approach back then at a time when it was really just starting to take hold of the game in England.

Before that, there had been a lot more emphasis on the character of players, work rate and desire.

We still had that, but now there was this tactical approach being overlaid on it and I think that stood us in good stead for the following few years.

Look, Brian Clough was an absolute legend of the game, possibly the best manager of all time.

So following him was a huge, huge task and Frank had to put his identity on the team.

He achieved that and did it very quickly in that first year.

I think Forest had looked at Stan Collymore previously, but Frank took the plunge and everyone knows what happened next.

He could spot great players and bring the best out of them; Stan, Bryan Roy, Lars Bohinen.

The season itself wasn't as straightforward as some people may remember.

Forest were a big scalp in that league and everyone wanted to beat us. There were also some big teams in the First Division that season; Wolves, Palace, Leicester, Middlesbrough, Sunderland, West Brom - all teams that wouldn't look out of place in the Premier League.

I think we actually only won three of our first dozen games and it was clear this wasn't going to be a walkover, not that we'd expected it to be. It was a high standard.

When I first arrived, I had to watch quite a few games from the sidelines.

Frank was actually quite apologetic about it, but he wanted me to watch and see how we were playing. That's how much thought he put into things.

He said: 'Bide your time and see how we're doing things, so that you'll know where you can have most impact when you get in.'

I'm not sure many managers would do that with new signings these days.

But he was right and it was good to get that perspective before stepping into the fray.

When I did get called upon, I got goals against Stoke and Bolton, but we still lost both games, 3-2 and 4-3.

I was starting to think my goals were a bit of a jinx, even though the one at Bolton was one I was particularly pleased with.

I didn't get many goals and they were rarely tap-ins or headers, but every now and then if I got just enough space, I could hit a ball cleanly and that one at the old Bolton ground flew in the top corner. It just kissed the underside of the bar as it went in - somehow that always makes them look more spectacular.

On the whole though, maybe we were a bit too open at first, but over a short period of time, we tightened up and things started to click for us.

We beat Notts County - I know the fans enjoyed that one - and at one point Stan was scoring more than a goal a game.

Scot Gemmill was chipping in, Woany could score spectacular goals from anywhere, Kingsley was having a great season on the wing and Colin Cooper and Stevie Chettle were solid as a rock in front of Mark Crossley.

Norm is a great guy, hell of a character and always had a funny story to tell. I don't think he's changed a bit down the years.

I think we went 13 games unbeaten at one point and we were stringing together runs of four or five wins on the trot.

When you get that momentum, the confidence is infectious and potential draws become wins and potential defeats become draws. You just find a way.

The prime example is the Peterborough game at the end of the season where we were 2-0 down against the bottom of the league.

There was an expectation there, but it wasn't just from everyone else looking in, it was from us the players, as well. We knew what we needed to do and even at 2-0 down, it was a case of 'OK, let's put this right'.

Obviously, it turned out to be a great occasion and we got there in the end. Just!

To get promotion back to the Premier League in that first season was just the stuff of dreams really - it couldn't have gone much better.

And to be named Player of the Year was the icing on the cake.

Not for everyone though. When it was announced at the award ceremony, I heard Stan just stood up and walked out of the place. Just went. I think he had a strop because he thought he was a shoo-in for it. I looked over and saw him go. Cheers mate!

That was Stan, God bless him. What can you say?

Enigma, maverick, call him what you like, but at the end of the day . . . Stan was Stan.

Later on I had to room with him on pre-season over in Norway.

Frank collared me and said: 'Look Dave, you're one of the more sensible ones, I want you to room with Stan and keep an eye on him.'

Let me just say that after about a day and a half . . . I was pleading to get out of that room.

I'm not sure he understood the meaning of the word curfew but he definitely knew the importance of using the fire exits when required.

But bizarrely, sharing that room ended up with me helping him write his transfer request out.

This was when Stan was trying to get to Liverpool, but he had no idea how to word things to the club.

I was like: *'Really? You seriously want to do this? And you want ME to help?'*

But he was so unhappy at that point, his mind was set on leaving.

I remember the club had lined up a horse-trotting event for us - a really good team-building night.

Stan just said: 'No, I'm not going.'

I said: 'You've got to go, it's a team thing.'

But if Stan didn't want to do something, he wasn't going to do it. That was the way he was.

When I got downstairs Liam said to me: 'Where's Stan?'

I had to tell a porky pie and say: 'Not a clue.'

So I don't know what he got up to instead, but he didn't want to be at Forest any more, that's for sure and that was sad because he was a good guy, really.

Of course, the main thing with Stan was . . . he was a fantastic player.

He was brilliant for Forest who made a big profit on him when he went to Liverpool and he did well there too.

Did he achieve as much in his career as his talent deserved? Well, only he can judge that.

I remember one time we played Millwall away and he scored and was taunting the home fans down there - not the brightest thing to do and they were completely wound up as the game went on.

I can still remember that time was coming up towards the end of the match and the ball got played towards the corner flag.

I went flying after the ball and as I was going one way, I saw the linesman running in the opposite direction.

I thought: *'What the hell's going on here? Where's he going?'*

I turned round and half the players were already down the tunnel - the ref had blown for full-time and the Millwall fans were on the pitch.

I thought: 'Oh my God, Stan - what have you done?'

I came to an abrupt stop, turned round and legged it back as fast as I could, dodging some very angry Cockneys on the way.

We hadn't even beaten them - it was a 2-2 draw - so God knows what it would have been like if we'd won.

I think that first season back in the Premier League with Stan and Bryan Roy was when we were at our strongest, not just in terms of personnel but also in terms of mindset - and that's a big thing.

It's a cliche, but winning is a good habit to get into and we came up with belief, not maybe that we were going to win the Premier League, but certainly that we were a good side.

Frank added well to the squad with Bryan Roy coming in. He was so quick, very bright and could do anything on the pitch, Bryan.

Maybe it was a hangover from his days in Italy back then, but he actually used to practice falling over in the opposition box. He had a technique to catch the defender's trailing leg to win free-kicks and penalties.

Maybe others do the same these days, but it was a new one on us! Great player though and a lovely, lovely man.

What's interesting is that if you look at the squad when we finished third, we really only used about 16 players.

I think I played all over the place during my time with Forest, but because we had a clear way of playing, it allowed Frank to do that and feel confident that people could slot in.

The core of the side played every week, there was no squad rotation and again, nearly everyone had been with us the year before, I think Bryan was our only new signing at that point.

So that shows the quality, the unity and the strength that we had to finish above the likes of Liverpool, Arsenal, Chelsea, etc.

We went the first eleven games unbeaten in the league and that gave us belief too. We drew with Manchester United, we beat Spurs and Everton - big clubs.

Bryan was showing his pedigree and formed a fantastic partnership with Stan and we were flying.

I think towards the end of that season we won nine out of ten games and drew the other.

We turned Sheffield Wednesday over 7-1 at Hillsborough on April Fool's Day and it was just an annihilation - one of the best team performances I've ever been involved in.

So yes, that was an achievement and I don't think any other team coming up from the Championship has ever matched that since.

For me, it was just a pleasure to be a part of, because we weren't doing this with any battering ram tactics, we were playing excellent football - the type befitting Nottingham Forest.

The club had to strengthen the following year when Stan left and to be fair, they tried.

Kevin Campbell came in and was a solid signing, you knew what you were getting.

But the one where we weren't sure what we'd got, even after he'd arrived, was Andrea Silenzi. We kept turning round and asking Frank: 'Are you *sure* he's not an ice cream salesman?'

He'd got good pedigree and had played with Maradona, even made the Italian national team.

I remember Pearcey and me talking to Frank about it some time afterwards and asking: 'What the hell happened?'

Frank gave out a sigh and admitted they'd bought him off watching videos - he'd never seen him play.

It's a scary thing; you can make anyone look good for a few minutes if you splice together all their best moments. But when they're nothing like that most of the time, you've got a problem.

Nothing against him personally. I think all the lads would say the same - he's a lovely fella and I got on really well with him and tried to make him feel welcome.

But could he do it in the English Premier League? No.

At times, he looked like a drunken horse - his feet were all over the place.

You can imagine what someone like Pearcey made of it all.

I love Stuart; I'd played against him before signing and it was always the same - the threats, the digs, everything you thought it was going to be when you were up against Stuart Pearce.

You had to stand up to that or he'd crush you.

It was all part of the banter back in the day - these days you wouldn't be able to get away with it, people would be rolling around on the floor, cameras would be picking up every word, it would be scandal after scandal, week after week.

But I took it on the chin with him and when I joined Forest we became great friends. After a while, you begin to see his softer side - yes, he does have one!

He commanded huge respect and the thing with him is, if HE said something was black, it was black. If he said it was white, it was white. There was no messing with him from the lads. He was the captain and the authority figure.

I remember one Christmas he decided we were all going to go to watch Madness over in Birmingham.

And not only that . . . we were to dress up in Madness gear, the suits, shades, etc.

Instead, me, Steve Chettle and Col Cooper turned up in dresses - don't ask me why! We just did it for the laugh.

Stu knew Suggs and the guys in the band so he said he'd get us in backstage after the gig.

Well, as so often is the case, that didn't happen so you've got us standing out behind this venue in Birmingham wearing dresses and of course . . . it started flipping snowing.

We were absolutely freezing and I'm not sure what Madness would have made of us three looking like drowned rats in dresses.

We all piled back on the bus and went out round Nottingham instead. It seemed like a good idea at the time (!) and we ended up having a great night.

*So if you saw three ugly sisters wearing dresses and covered in snow one night back in the 90s . . . yes, that was us!*

*

Back on the pitch, we started my third season with the club well in 1995/96.

I think we were unbeaten in the league again for the first 12 games or so, which was a testament to how well prepared we were.

It was stop-start for me though as I'd tweaked a hamstring so missed two or three of the big European games, which was really frustrating.

Frank was having me on the bench just in case I was needed but it wasn't right. I ended up playing in a reserve game to see how it was and it just went, so that was a blow.

I managed to get back in time for the Bayern Munich games and playing in that Olympic Stadium was a really memorable night for me.

As my dad was in the RAF, we lived in Holland for a few years and I was actually born in Germany. Bayern was always one of those clubs that I followed, not just because they were a big team but because of the great players they'd had; Beckenbauer, Rummenigge, etc.

So for me to go and play in that World Cup final stadium that I'd seen so often as a child was a big thing. I know their new stadium is fantastic and state of the art, but there was something special about the old one; the floodlights, the history, Forest winning the European Cup there.

Jurgen Klinsmann scored and I think they thought it was going to be a formality against us in that first leg. No chance.

Within a minute or so, we got a free-kick and lined up for one of our set plays.

It wasn't ground-breaking or anything - just get the ball deep to Chetts who would nod it back across the middle for someone to get on the end of.

Instead, I probably hit it a bit too deep, Oliver Kahn either left it or got underneath it and as Steve craned his neck to get it back, the angle was perfect to drop into the net.

For a split second, you could hear nothing. It was like something off a film.

The home fans had still been celebrating their goal when suddenly, this team from Nottingham had the cheek to score against them in their own back yard.

Then it was just this almighty roar from the thousands of Nottingham fans who'd made the journey.

Just a wonderful moment and it was great that Chetts scored because he's Forest through and through.

After that, I think they treated us with a lot more caution and knew they were in a game.

We ended up losing 2-1 but in Europe, with an away goal, it was a good result - especially against a team of Bayern's calibre.

Our issue was that we then wanted to have a pop at them at our place, go toe-to-toe with our fans behind us and with hindsight . . . that was completely the wrong thing to do.

Having said that, we started really well and had a couple of good chances in that first half.

If just one of those had gone in, we'd have had them where we wanted them.

Instead, very unusually, Norm made a bit of a hash of a free-kick and that put them 3-1 up with an away goal.

When that goal went it, it was just deflating. You could feel it in the stadium.

The way they worked then, they were so efficient, the pendulum really swung their way and they ended up hitting us for five, partly because we had to go looking for goals and that left space they could exploit.

They were such a good team though and deservedly went on to win the competition that year.

We weren't starstruck or anything though. There was plenty of quality in our team, people who'd played internationals - I played 62 games for Wales - so we'd come across top players before.

And they were fine after the game, we wished them luck and I think there was a great deal of respect for Nottingham Forest even though we'd been well beaten.

We finished ninth in that season, we reached the FA Cup quarter final and also had that good run in the UEFA Cup so it was respectable overall and there was no sign of trouble on the horizon.

If anything, we were looking to improve our league position without the distraction of Europe.

But, well, what happened is on the record books.

I don't think there's any one single reason for Forest being relegated, it was a combination of things.

We weren't scoring enough goals and we weren't tight enough at the back.

We brought in the Croatian Nikola Jerkan on the back of a good Euro 96 and he was the smelliest player I ever came across.

Seriously, he ALWAYS smelled of cheese - I've never whiffed anything like it. I think he only lasted a year and you know when someone says there was a sigh of relief when he went? Yes there flipping was. Nice guy, but . . *blimey!*

Kingsley went to Grimsby and personally, I was going through an acrimonious divorce during that last season I was there.

Obviously, that's not particularly nice for anyone. Frank knew about it and was very supportive, but it wasn't a great period of my life and inevitably, I had thoughts and issues away from football.

It's hard when that happens to anyone in any walk of life and I'm sure anyone who's been through it will know what I'm talking about.

When it's football and you have to perform every week in front of thousands of people, there's more scrutiny than normal and you feel that too.

Footballers are human and major personal issues inevitably have an effect.

Either way, the team wasn't getting results and one way or another Frank was relieved of his duties, which was a really sad time for me.

We'll never know what would have happened if he had stayed, but with his record at the club up to that point you'd think he would have been given more of a chance at it.

Pearcey did what he could for a while, then Dave Bassett came in and, quite frankly, he was never one of my favourites. And probably vice versa.

It was clear that Dave wasn't really keen on me as a player and if you think about it, I was never really is style.

He was very direct and very defence-minded, but for the players we had in that relegation season, it obviously didn't work.

Dean Saunders was there with us at the time and he's a real character, Deano - on and off the pitch. He's really good at impressions and taking the Mick out of other people.

I remember sitting in the dressing room one time and Deano was just getting into his stride doing a classic take-off of Harry Bassett

I don't know if you've spotted this, but Harry somehow doesn't breathe when he talks. He's rattling away so quickly and you're thinking: 'How is he breathing?'

So Dean was like: *'Oirightwegetdahntherightsidegetdahntheleftside getitupthemiddle'* and we were all cracking up.

Then I looked up and saw that Dave was coming down the corridor and he could hear the whole thing.

I tried to shut Deano up but by then he was in full flow and the lads were in hysterics.

Fair play to Dave Bassett because he burst into the dressing room and said: *'OiDeanoIdontalklikethatItalklikethis!'*

So there was nothing wrong with our team spirit or desire that season, but Dean's an example of where nothing was going right on the pitch for us that year.

I knew him from the Wales squad and he's a great guy, a top player and on paper a very solid Premier League signing at that time.

But it just didn't happen for him at Forest, for whatever reason.

Steve Beaglehole and Richard Money came in to do some training and it was very much an emphasis on keeping it tight at the back. Any team needs that, but we needed wins at that stage.

We bought Pierre Van Hooijdonk late in the day, but by then it was a last throw of the dice and by the time he got used to the Premier League, it was really all over.

Getting relegated was painful, really painful.

No player wants to experience it and when you get back in that dressing room when it's all over, it's as low as it gets.

The only silver lining for the club on the horizon was that Dave Bassett had the experience of getting clubs out of the division below and that obviously stood Forest in good stead the following season.

For me, from a personal perspective, it was clear my time was coming to the end sadly.

I was limited to a couple of League Cup appearances. When that happens, you know the writing's on the wall.

I'd had four and a bit good years at the City Ground though and think I gave good value for the fee.

The last few months were very difficult because it was clear I wasn't going to play, but on the other hand, it was good to see the club doing so well and setting course for an immediate return to the Premier League.

By that time I was the *'wrong side of 34'*, but still not ready to call it a day at that level.

The chairman at Forest - Fred Reacher - had been great with me and when the opportunity came to go to Huddersfield things went through smoothly.

There was no animosity on either side and I've nothing but warm feelings towards Forest to this day. I was sad to leave, but in the circumstances, it was the best for everyone involved.

I was absolutely chuffed when they went back up as Champions that year - it was a fantastic achievement by the boys.

Me? I played quite a few games for Huddersfield that season and helped them stay up in the league, before brief spells at Lincoln and finally Stevenage.

I'd played around 700 games and was 37 when I finally stopped playing, so that's a good age for any player to get to and I look back on my career with great pride, winning the FA Cup with Coventry, playing for Wales and being part of some great clubs.

Obviously, there are highs and lows at every club you go to, but my time at Forest was fantastic overall.

The people were so friendly, the football we played was great to be a part of and it's just a brilliant club.

I still go back every now and again as a guest in the lounges at games and I love it - there's so much warmth about the place and the passion for the club burns as brightly as ever.

I was really disappointed to see them fall away recently when it looked like they had a real shot at a return to the Premier League.

That's where the club deserves to be and I hope Forest get back there soon.

*They've been away too long.*

CHAPTER 4

# MARK CROSSLEY: LUCKY FOR SOME

Thirteen's an unlucky number isn't it? Even at school in Barnsley you learn about that. (And chips. And gravy. Peas, if you went somewhere posh.)

It's not unlucky for me though, 13, and if you stick around to the end of this chapter you'll find out why.

On the way, I'll try to keep you entertained, educated and informed about my career at Nottingham Forest.

And if I miss any bits out, it's because I'm playing golf in a bit and I don't want to be late teeing off. *Deal?* Right, let's get cracking.

A long time ago, when I could still play football and I was just a spotty young lad, my dad helped set up a team called Hoyland Common Falcons.

Seeing as I was in the school team, I made it into their line-up too. And it wasn't just because my dad was on the committee. Honest.

With my athletic frame and high jumping ability there was only one position for me wasn't there? Yep - centre half.

But one day when I was 15, the goalkeeper was injured and my dad put me 'in the nets', simply because I was the biggest. And, well, there was nobody else.

So from that day on, I've never moved from goal - apart from that time I went up front and scored for Sheffield Wednesday, but even then, I still had my goalkeeping shirt and gloves on. (Look it up on YouTube if you don't believe it; back post, last minute, get in!)

Anyway, me going in goal was serendipitous - it was something that was just meant to happen - and I never looked back. If you're wondering how I know the word 'serendipitous' the bloke writing this down came up with it. *(Thanks, Keith.)*

The team was quite successful and there were quite a few scouts around looking at us young lads. Watford invited me down for a trial, where I did well and got offered a scholarship.

I was stopping in a house with David and Dean Holdsworth and - nothing against those lads - but I got homesick. You get like that when you're too far away from Barnsley and I just didn't like it.

I was only a young lad, straight out of school, so I knocked it on the head and came home.

Back in the 'real world', I signed up for a painting and decorating course at the local art and design college and that could have been it for me at that point. I had to get a trade lined up and find a 'proper' job.

Football-wise, I started playing for one of the local men's teams in the Sunday league - Hoyland Town Jaguars. They don't mess around with team names round Hoyland; *Falcons, Jaguars,* we've got the lot.

Really, we were the best team in the area and reached a major cup final at Bramall Lane - so this was a big thing for us - and again there were a few scouts came along to watch.

We won the cup and luckily for me, a Forest scout called Jack Noble came along and introduced me to Alan Hill. I was still only about 17 and next thing, I was lined up for a trial and then got offered another scholarship, this time at Forest.

It was absolutely brilliant for me, as it was a lot nearer than Watford and I could get up and down quite easily. I also understood the accent a bit better. So that was the end of my painting and decorating days. I put my brushes down. Football was back on and the rest, as they say, is history.

*

People often ask when was the first time I met Brian Clough - no matter who you are, it's not something you forget.

Me? Well, before I signed properly, I used to play for a team called Forest Colts; a guy called Mick Rayner was in charge and often, Cloughie used to come and watch.

He came down to one game where I did really well and at the end, he pulled me to one side. Obviously, he was one of the most famous and successful managers in the game by then so I was all ears, wondering what pearls of wisdom the great man was going to give me.

Would it be kicking and distribution? Handling? Positioning on crosses?

*Err, no*.

'Young man,' he said, 'If you want to come and play football for me . . . I suggest you get your hair cut.'

That was that. I had this big shaggy mess of hair at the time and the next day I was first in the queue at the barbers for a short back and sides. It was the start of a long and happy relationship where he told me to do something and I did it. Simple as that.

The man management of the guy was incredible. He just knew exactly what to say and do to get the best out of people. Even if it was just getting a haircut.

And often, it was with very few words. Or a look. Or maybe a swipe of a tennis racket that he carried around.

Either way, I got taken on properly by Forest and was fifth choice goalkeeper. If there was literally no-one else, it would have to be me.

What could possibly go wrong?

For me to get in the team, so many things would have to line up, it would need to be absolute serendipity. *(Thanks. Again.)*

Hans Segers would have to be out on loan somewhere, Paul Crichton and Darren Hayes would need to be injured and Steve Sutton would need to go down with a virus on the day of the game, too late for the club to get anyone else in.

*I mean, what are the chances?*

And yet on October 26, 1989 my parents got a call at home to get to the ground . . . because I was making my debut against Liverpool that night.

BUT (and as you can see, it's a big *BUT*) I didn't know in advance and they were told not to tell me either, because Cloughie thought that if I knew . . . I'd probably crap my pants.

As ever, he was absolutely right - I probably would have.

After all, it was only John Barnes, Peter Beardsley and Ian Rush up front for them, with Kenny Dalglish in the dugout.

At the time, I was living in digs with about ten other lads in Colwick Road and we strolled down to the ground, taking in the local fish and chip shop on the way for a chippy tea - as you do when you don't think you're going to be playing football against Liverpool in a few hours' time.

When we got to the stadium, I still had no idea I was playing so I was getting on with the normal jobs, bit of fetching and carrying, things like that.

My job that night was to turn the heating up full blast in the Liverpool dressing room so they'd all be a bit hot and sweaty before the game started. It was meant to dehydrate them and it was funny as anything seeing King Kenny coming out of their dressing room before kick-off, sweating cobs and asking for the heat to be turned down a touch.

Me *(with a straight face)*: 'Too hot?? I've no idea how that's happened but of course I'll sort it out for you, no problem Mr Dalglish.'

The other thing I had to do was clean Ian Bowyer's boots and make sure they were all ready for him.

So at about seven o'clock, I was just in the boot room sorting them out when I heard Cloughie in the corridor calling my name.

Well, it wasn't actually my name, it was one of his many nicknames for me - 'Sh*thouse'.

I thought: 'Blimey, what does he want me for?'

So I looked out into the corridor and he said those fateful words: 'Son, get your boots on. Get your gloves on . . . you're playing.'

That was that. It wasn't a wind-up. All those things that had to happen *had* happened and I was in. Oh my God.

I tell you what, he wasn't far off when he said I might crap my pants.

Suddenly those fish and chips on the way to the ground didn't seem like such a good idea - but at least I only had 45 minutes to worry about it.

I actually had to borrow some gloves because mine were a bit tattered. I went out for a warm-up under the lights, the crowd all murmuring and I just started to try to take it all in.

There were no goalkeeping coaches back then, just Brian Rice having a bit of a kick-in with me at the Trent End and a lot of Forest fans wondering who the hell I was. *Right, nice and easy Brian, I'll throw it to you and you volley it back to me.*

You've all seen it done a thousand times in warm-ups.

First one? Yep, straight through my hands.

I could hear the groan from the fans behind me and I thought: 'Well, that's a *great* start!'

When the game got going, the funny thing is, I can't remember much of it, but I can remember my first touch.

The ball had gone out and I always had a really long kick on me - it was one of the biggest strengths in my armoury. So I thought: 'Right everyone, watch this.'

I lined the ball up, took a run and - *boom* - sent it virtually the length of the pitch. It got a big *'ooooo'* from the home fans and that gave me a lot of confidence. I don't think there was ever anything so much riding on a kick - imagine if I'd slipped on my backside. That might have been that.

But I thought: 'Right, no worries, if it comes near me, I'll just kick it as far as I can.'

So that's what I did at every opportunity. They can't score from 50 yards away, can they?

Well, maybe John Barnes could. But he didn't that night.

Luckily, the lads played really well and I didn't have a lot to do. Maybe they were doing everything they could to protect me and if so, cheers!

But I got through it and most importantly, we got a result. At the end, my smile? Big? Blimey. *Like a Cheshire cat.*

I'd played a professional game of football at 18, for Nottingham Forest, against that Liverpool side and we'd won. It was just the stuff dreams are made of, it really was.

But that wasn't the end of it.

After the game, amid all the euphoria *(I came up with that one myself)*, the gaffer grabbed me and asked me to come with him to the referee's room. I thought it might just be something routine, that I was unaware of.

Anyway, we got in there and Cloughie says: 'Referee, it's been this young man's debut tonight, he's played very well and I'd like the match ball for him please.'

I don't think the ref knew what to do, but this was obviously not something routine.

He looked a bit nervous this ref, and he said: *'I-I-I can't do that, Mr Clough. He's not scored a hat-trick or anything and it's against regulations . . .'*

At which point, unbelievably, the gaffer snatched the ball out of his hands, threw it at me and said: 'Sh*thouse, bugger off with that ball - *quick!'*

I don't think the ref knew what to do. I mean, what would *you* do?

It's Brian Clough. You're in the City Ground. He doesn't just rule the roost, he MAKES the rules. And the roost.

So that's how I got the match ball from my first game.

Chuffed to bits, I went back to our dressing room and got all the lads to sign it for me. I thought that would be that - a great souvenir that I'd keep forever. Absolutely delighted.

But then the gaffer came in and said: 'Well done lad . . . now, go and knock on the Liverpool door and get them to sign it as well.'

I was like *'hold on'* (although obviously, I didn't say those words out loud).

I thought: 'Flaming 'eck. We've just beat Liverpool 2-1 and now he wants ME, an 18-year-old nobody to go to their dressing room and ask

Kenny Dalglish - KENNY DALGLISH - if I could get Ian Rush, John Barnes and all these megastars to sign this ball for me.'

I was absolutely bricking it, so quick-as-a-flash, I came up with a plan.

I'd go half way down the corridor, turn round, come back and say they wouldn't do it.

So that's what I did. I set off, got half way, turned round . . . and there was Cloughie, leaning out of our dressing room, watching every step I made.

*'Knock on the door, Sh*thouse,' he said, 'Knock on the door.'*

*Gulp*. Bang, bang, bang and the door opened. Fair play to Kenny Dalglish, because even though they'd been beaten, he let me in and got all their players to sign it.

He knew it was my debut and he was an absolute class act. All those Liverpool lads were. Mind you, I didn't hang around to check if the heating was still alright for them.

So that's a fantastic 'first game' memory for me; I've still got the ball somewhere. It's one of those yellow Mitre ones with a bit of a stripe on it.

Most of the signatures have faded now but I can still make one or two out. The thing is, I know who signed it that night, so it doesn't matter.

I know what it means to me and how lucky I was to get that opportunity.

I've given away a lot of memorabilia and most of my shirts, gloves and things down the years to charity, because if something good can come from them then that's better than them just sitting up in my loft.

But some things I've kept hold of and that ball is one of them.

*

I played against Newcastle in the next game and did OK as we won again up at their place, Lee Chapman scored.

I can't remember if that was the game, but one time we played up at St James' Park and the home fans really got into me about something - no idea what, but there were coins galore coming down onto the pitch aimed at me. Who'd have thought those Geordies would have so much loose change hanging around?

In the end, when the ball went out of play, I scooped up as much as I could and gave it to the ball boy as a bit of a cash bonus.

I jogged back to the nets and just gave the home fans a big smile and a thumbs up to the Gallowgate End.

After that it calmed down a bit - I think if you're OK with fans they'll be OK back and you can have a bit of fun with them during the game sometimes. You've just got to pick your away grounds carefully (!).

I used to get a lot of stick off Derby fans, but I've always been the type of character who gave it back anyway. If you can't take it, don't hand it out, that's what I always say - to fans and players.

You always get the old 'yoooou fat b******' when you take a goal kick and me especially, as I always struggled with my weight at times - it was always up and down.

When I go round different places now, I meet some of the fans from back then and they always say how they used to enjoy it if I ever gave them grief back.

You don't get too much of that these days; everyone's worried about ending up on an FA charge or something, but back then you could have banter with the fans and it was all part of going to the match.

The next game after that was a league cup tie against Coventry and although we won 3-2, I made my first mistake really and one of their goals was down to me.

If I thought I was getting established, I had a bit of a shock coming.

Cloughie and all the management team had a way of keeping everyone in line - no-one was ever allowed to get too big for their boots.

Pearcey, Neil Webb, even his own son Nigel - all England internationals. But if ever he thought anyone was in danger of getting too big for their boots, he'd be on it like a flash.

In my case, it was after the game on a Saturday when I said to the lads 'see you Monday'.

The gaffer heard this and said: 'Where are you going tonight son?'

'I'm going back to Barnsley, gaffer.'

He looked at me and said: 'My house. Nine o'clock tomorrow morning. Bring your gloves. Don't be late.'

Well first off, I had no idea where he lived. So I had to track down one of the ground staff to take me out there in his van.

When we arrived, he shot off and left me there in the kitchen with Cloughie's wife Barbara.

His brilliant dog, Del Boy, was keeping an eye on me, sniffing at my crotch and whatnot, but you daren't shoo him away - it's Cloughie's dog, he can do what he wants *(within reason)*.

Eventually, the gaffer appeared and said: 'Thank you, for agreeing to play for my son Simon's team this morning.'

Oh. Right.

I thought: *'Eh? What's going on?'*

But, of course, the words that came out of my mouth were: *'No problem, gaffer.'*

So that was that. Simon ran a team called AC Hunters in the Derbyshire Sunday League and so I went from playing against Liverpool and Newcastle to some muddy pitch covered in God knows what on a Sunday morning in front of two men and a dog.

It was only when we'd been playing for a bit that I looked across and realised Archie Gemmill was running the line (!). European Cup winner, World Cup legend, top man - and there he was helping out Cloughie's son's team on a freezing Sunday morning the pub league.

It did the trick of keeping my feet on the ground though, especially after the club got fined £50 for fielding a ringer - and Cloughie made *me* pay it for the privilege of helping out.

It was a lot of money in those days and come to think of it, it still is, isn't it? *Fifty quid*. Ouch.

Almost as a side note, after that Coventry game, Sutty recovered and I never got a sniff of the first team for the rest of that season. I was back to the reserves.

It was the same story the following year too. Steve was a great keeper and clear first choice, while I was definitely still a young lad learning my trade.

I only came in if he was unavailable for some reason, but did play two games in a week up in Manchester against United and City.

We lost 1-0 to United but beat City 3-0 at Maine Road.

What's interesting looking back is that I think there were only 34,000 at Old Trafford and 26,000 at City. People talk about the good old days, but in the 1980s crowds were a lot smaller than they were today.

Mind you, in Manchester you'll probably have 50,000 who swear they were at those games. *(Yeah, right - course you were.)*

It wasn't until the 1990/91 season that I became first choice and I'm proud to say that I played in every league game that year.

I think we were a settled side and there wasn't 'squad rotation' or anything like that. You had your team and most weeks that was who played. It was the same at every club really. There were only two subs allowed, so squads were a lot tighter.

At the back there was me, Pearcey, Brian Laws, Stevie Chettle and Des Walker and I'll put that back four against any you choose to mention; unbelievable players and it was a joy to be in goals behind those lads.

Obviously, we got to the FA Cup Final that year and that was just an incredible experience. I was only 21 and you pinch yourself at it all, you really do. That was always THE big game growing up, wasn't it?

Back then, it was probably the only live game on TV all year, along with England against Scotland in the Home Internationals.

Always the same two or three commentators too - John Motson and Barry Davies on the BBC or Brian Moore on ITV.

The country would come to a standstill for the Cup Final and we were desperate to win it for the gaffer as it was the only trophy he hadn't won.

*You might not be aware of that - if you'd been living on Mars.*

After all, it was the only thing the press and TV ever mentioned: 'Do you know it's the only trophy your manager's never won in his career?'

Believe it or not, mate . . . *yes*.

Obviously, people remember it for the Gazza tackle, Pearcey's free-kick and Des's own goal, but the penalty save I made from Gary Lineker often gets forgotten. *(Not by me, obviously.)*

I think it's because we were on the losing side. Dave Beasant famously saved from John Aldridge, but people remember that because Wimbledon won it that year.

When you get beat, it's a bit lost. But for me, to be one of only three people to save a penalty in the Cup Final - Peter Cech is the other - is again, something I look back on with pride.

I've lost count how many times I've watched it. It's one repeat I never get bored of. To be honest, when I brought their lad down I was in a bit of a panic that the ref might send me off, because there was a new rule about red cards for professional fouls that year.

So I was saying: 'I got the ball ref! Never a penalty in a million years!'

Really, I was saying anything to avoid being sent off and thankfully it worked.

It's funny when you're a keeper on a penalty, because you can't really lose, can you? You're the hero if you save it and if they score, well, they've had a free shot haven't they?

The funny thing is, I could see Lineker rubbing his nose a bit, looking a bit off, no eye contact or anything, and I thought: 'Oh aye? He's bit nervous here.'

So you try to delay it, make a fuss, do anything you can to up the pressure just a bit more. How's your bottle son?

*It's only the FA Cup Final - Wembley, 90,000 here, shown live in 80 countries, eyes of millions all around the world on you . . . no pressure!*

And then - *bang* - good hand to it, out for a corner and we're still one-up. To be honest, while I was absolutely buzzing, I had to keep concentrating up. Imagine if they'd scored from the corner.

The lads were all congratulating me but I was more worried about a quick cross coming in: 'Gerroff! Get set for the corner! Come on!'

That's genuinely what I was thinking.

Everyone knows what happened next, there's not much to say, other than a great player like Des didn't deserve to concede a goal like that - an absolute fluke.

I just wish we'd have won. If it had been a case of him scoring the penalty but us winning the trophy in the end, I'd swap in the blink of an eye - that goes without saying. It's all about the team.

Afterwards, well . . . everything was just flat, everyone was down, just very quiet in the dressing room. It was one of the most memorable finals of the past 40 years probably and we'd played a part in it.

Normally no-one remembers the losers in Cup Finals, but everyone remembers Forest from that year.

We lost though and that was the biggest thing. Just sheer disappointment. It still hurts.

But you've got to get up and go again and that's what we did.

*I do a lot of after dinner speaking and events these days and love talking about the old days and what I consider to be one of football's best eras - the 1990s.*

*It's not just because I was playing back then, but I think it was a great period for the English game.*

*At those events, people sometimes ask whether I've got any regrets about my career and I'll be honest, yes, I do.*

*Whenever I let anyone down, I've always regretted it. Not just for myself, but mainly for my family, friends and people who'd put their faith in me.*

*When I was younger, I was a bit of a rogue and being in the public eye from an early age, some people - not many, but some - tended to get a little bit jealous. There'd sometimes be flashpoint on nights out and I wasn't one to really stand down, that wasn't in my nature back then. So that got me in a bit of trouble with the law. I got in an altercation one night when I shouldn't have been out, because it was a couple of nights before a game.*

*I ended up getting pushed through a chip shop window - before you ask, the chippy was closed at the time - and I paid a heavy price for that.*

*The press got hold of the story, twisted it, blew it up out of all proportion and the upshot was I missed two Wembley finals, the ZDS and the League Cup against Manchester United.*

*No matter how much money I was fined, it doesn't compare with missing out on those big games and knowing I'd let people down.*

*So yes, that's my biggest regret. It didn't happen too often, but when it did it was pretty big unfortunately. Sometimes you have to just make these mistakes along the way and learn from them.*

*The thing is, friends and people who know me well say I'm a bit like a light switch. I can be the most laid back bloke in the world - quite lovely, some people would say - but I can't stand bullies and if someone says something, I'm not one to walk away.*

*Something would flick in me like a light switch and that would be that. Trouble, stupid trouble.*

*Thankfully, I think I've matured, grown up, whatever, as the years have gone by and in recent years, I've come to focus more on mental health.*

*These days, I do a lot of walking and find that really helps. Try it and you'll see.*

*If anyone knows about #walkingsbrilliant then they'll know that's gone to another level in recent times and I'm hoping to climb Kilimanjaro next year so that's another level again - literally.*

*I'm really, really happy in life at the moment and I just hope that anything I do helps people to get out, get fitter and be happier physically and mentally.*

*It sounds like a small thing, but it's so good to be able to talk to someone, anyone about things and hopefully more people will come to see that it's OK to talk about feelings and what's going on inside people's minds.*

*There's nothing soft about it - we've all got to look after each other in this life and everyone needs a bit of support along the way sometimes.*

The following season Teddy Sheringham came in, Roy Keane really made his mark and we were eighth for the second year running.

Funnily enough, a few years later, I saved three penalties against Spurs down at their place in a Fifth Round match. You may remember this. I do.

Pearcey scored the first for us and luckily Ian Walker went the wrong way, never got near it.

I say 'luckily' because when Stuart was hitting them in training, sometimes you'd just get out of the way because they were that hard, if you got a hand to one, it would bend your fingers back and hurt like hell.

Ian Woan's nearly broke the net that night at Spurs and Chetts' was absolutely banged in too. We had some brilliant penalty takers at Forest.

Teddy took the last one for them, the decider to keep them in it, and as I walked past him to take my place I just said: *'Don't forget, I know where you put them.'*

Ted, who took the longest run-up you've ever seen, looked like he ignored me and whether it had any effect, I don't know . . .

. . . but I *do* know I saved it.

Then that was it wasn't it? I broke my own land speed record to get down the other end and celebrate with the Forest fans, knees up around my chest, with all the lads chasing me like a whippet.

Maybe it was the save, or maybe it was the goatee beard I was sporting that night, but suddenly everyone wanted to pile on top of me. (I'm hoping it was the first.)

At the time, the big goal celebration of the day was the *Klinsmann dive*. Me? I turned it into the *Crossley Flop*. Splat. Loved it.

Now be fair, I'd just played 120 minutes and run the entire length of the pitch so maybe it wasn't the most athletic dive you've ever seen as I launched myself onto the floor, taking out a big chunk of the pitch with me. But when it's a game like that, who cares? *(Apparently, Alan Sugar did. He sent me a bill for £50 to repair the divot!)*

The other penalty I'm most asked about is the save from Matt Le Tissier. I say *the* save because it's the only one he ever missed - what a player, an unbelievable talent.

I think Carl Tiler had given the penalty away but there was no special plan for saving it - I always went with my gut instinct.

Later on, I did study people but in those early days it was just make your mind up, commit and try to get something on it. Even if you've gone the wrong way, stick a leg out and if it goes down the middle, you've got a chance.

That's what happened that day and I managed to get hands to it, but it still popped back to Le Tiss on the follow-up.

I don't know if he was surprised that he hadn't scored but whatever happened, he missed the rebound too. So out of 48 spot-kicks, he only ever missed one - and I saved it. Again, that's something to be proud of, because like I say, he was an unbelievable player as his record shows.

Funnily enough though, that's not the end of the story.

They absolutely worship him down in Southampton and a few years ago, he was inducted into their hall of fame with a big do at a theatre down there. As you can imagine, it was packed to the rafters, I think Dan Walker was hosting the event and all his old Saints managers were there paying tribute to Le Tiss.

What he didn't know is that the organisers had given me a shout and asked me to go down and recreate the penalty save as a surprise, right at the end of the evening.

I had my full kit and gloves on behind this curtain at the back of the stage where they'd set up goalposts and were going to give him the chance to put things right by scoring against me.

So I was watching from behind the scenes and he didn't even know I was there. It was a fantastic night and at the end, Dan Walker talked to him about that miss and said: *'Well, we're going to give you a chance to redeem yourself . . .'*

They pulled the curtain back - and there I was.

Matt was brilliant about it all and I think he definitely wanted to score. Some people might think I'd let him on his big night.

Me? *Nah. I saved it again.*

The place just burst into laughter and cheers and Le Tiss was cracking up too. Great lad, great night. Maybe the fact he was wearing shoes and the goals may not have been full size had something to do with it, but I'm still counting it as a save (another one).

Matt was a great example of sheer natural talent and, like me, he was playing at a time when the first nutritionists started to come into the game.

At Forest, if we were away, a pre-match meal on a Saturday used to be beans on toast or scrambled eggs. The type of thing that hadn't changed for years I think.

If we were in Nottingham on a Friday, we always used to go to Antonio's at the top of the road and it was steak and chips all round.

I'm not sure what the sports scientists today would have made of that, but it was great for us.

*

The game was definitely changing over the 1990s and while it was a memorable decade for Forest, it was a turbulent one too.

Obviously, Brian Clough retired in the season we got relegated and that was unbefitting a man of his stature - a terrible time all round.

I think everyone who'd ever been managed by him or had worked with him at Forest loved the man.

I just felt it was a privilege to be in his company; to learn from him about values, morals, the way to live your life and conduct yourself.

It was more than just football with the gaffer, he was absolutely inspirational in life itself.

People now who just met him in passing can almost eat out on that fact alone: 'What? You *met* Brian Clough?'

So to get to work with him up close for so many years was just a huge, huge privilege. It really was.

People ask if he'd be able to cope in the modern era when all the top players are millionaires and clubs have become massive businesses and commodities.

He would cope, trust me.

He would still have that ability to get people to run through brick walls for him. He'd still know the game. He'd know how to win. He'd still be Brian Clough. He'd probably be Prime Minister by now.

Come to think of it, that might not be a bad thing!

When the great man stepped down though, Frank Clark was a top appointment by the club. A Forest legend through and through and that period where we came straight back up then finished third in the Premier League, then played in the UEFA Cup was just an amazing time to be at the club.

We weren't big-headed or anything, but we were a good side and we knew if we got in our stride, we could give people a good pasting.

Stan Collymore and Bryan Roy forged a brilliant partnership up front, they were both so skilful and sharp - even in training you'd be thinking: 'Well, he's not going to shoot from there' and then a split-second later the ball would be whizzing towards your head.

We beat Manchester United at Old Trafford and then put seven past Sheffield Wednesday at Hillsborough, which was unbelievable, especially as they had Des Walker playing for them that day.

At one point, I was stood there thinking: 'What score is it now?' It was so crazy, I lost count.

The following season, I loved that European campaign so much; going on all those trips, seeing different places, playing Bayern Munich home and away.

I think the secret to our success over that spell was that we had no fear. We had a plan and we stuck to it and we frustrated the hell out of people.

Frank had us so well organised that we just closed up space everywhere on the pitch, then hit people on the break. It was the type of thing European teams had done for years, but now we were doing it to them.

I know the Forest fans loved those trips, especially some of the older lads who'd been to the Olympic Stadium when Forest won the European Cup. It must have been brilliant for them to go back there again, especially as Bayern have now moved grounds, so it was a last chance really.

I know we got beat 2-1 but we held our heads up high, even in the second leg too. They knew they'd been in a game and the name 'Nottingham Forest' was back in European circles.

I played a lot for Wales *(well, I was in the squad a lot)* and wherever you went, people always knew the Forest name. You never had to explain to anyone what the club was. Wherever you were and whatever language they spoke, people recognised it straight away - then normally said: *'Oh yes - Brian Clough!'*

Obviously, things were up and down (literally) for Forest in the late 90s but I never really came close to leaving.

The only time it was a possibility really was just around the time Frank took over and Leeds United came in with an offer that the club accepted.

I wasn't a Leeds fan, but my dad used to take me to watch them sometimes when I was a kid, as they were the best side around back then.

That was before I got a bit older and realised we could get in to see Barnsley for free by climbing over the wall. But I wasn't really a fan of either team growing up - and I'm proper Forest now, obviously.

Anyway, Leeds came in for me while we were on an end of season trip and Fred Reacher rang me up and asked if I'd heard about it. I genuinely hadn't, but the next thing he said was the club had agreed a fee - it was about £2.5 million, big money at the time.

He said: 'Listen Norm, we've agreed the fee not because we want you to go, but because we could do with the money and we could invest it elsewhere.

'But whatever they offer you, come back to me and if we can match it, we will.'

So I went up there and they offered me a really good contract, but I was torn because I didn't want to leave, even though we'd just been relegated. I wanted to stay and help the club get back.

I didn't sign anything up there, rang Fred back and, while he couldn't match Leeds' offer, the club offered me a new contract and that was good enough for me.

And I never, ever regretted it.

If I'd have had my way, I'd have played my entire career at Forest - that was one of my aims really, to be a one-club man at such a great club.

I didn't quite manage it, but I did stay long enough for one of the biggest nights of my career.

It wasn't a competitive game at all - it was my testimonial at the City Ground in May, 2000.

If you were there, thank you from the bottom of my heart. People ask me about it and all I can say it was magical, but it took so much organising that the night itself seemed to go by in a flash.

So many special people turned out on the night, it was just well, mind-blowing really.

*If I could hit pause and just take it all in again for a few moments, I would do it in the blink of an eye.*

There was such a good turnout of supporters, family, friends and players from my Forest career and from other teams, I was just so touched.

And, best of all, the gaffer came, too.

*I mean, talk about special.*

I know he wasn't in the best of health at that point but I knew he had a driver and his mate was called Colin. I got hold of him and said: 'Look, is there any chance of getting the gaffer to the game? If he's not up to it, no problem, but we'd love him to come down.'

He smiled and said: 'Well, why don't you take your kids and go and see him at his house and ask him.'

I said: 'Really, do you think he'd mind?'

'No, he'll be fine. Just go and ask.'

So I gathered up my kids, made my way over to Cloughie's house and knocked on the door. Barbara answered and was very nice as always and I could see the gaffer, popping his head up behind her.

Before I could speak, he said: 'Sh*thouse . . . the answer's yes.

*'Now get off my land.'*

I didn't even have time to thank him.

But just as he turned to go inside, he looked back for a moment and said: 'That can't be your daughter because she's beautiful - and you're ugly.'

He was right (as usual) and that was that.

We couldn't advertise his presence in the build-up to the night, because it was hard to say whether he'd be up to coming until nearer the time.

But once we got the shout the day before that he was definitely going to make an appearance, the response in Nottingham and beyond was just unbelievable.

It says a lot that thousands of people would turn out just to see the great man, years after he'd retired. And he would turn out for me. It's just so, so humbling and also amazing.

I remember being in the dressing room beforehand and the police coming in and saying: 'Sorry Mark, we're going to have to put the kick-off back - they're queueing over the Trent bridge.'

*I'll be honest, that was a great feeling for me. Lump in the throat time. A very proud night indeed.*

Not only that, but for Brian Clough to walk out with the European Cup-winning team . . . well, it gives me goosebumps just thinking about it, even now 20 years later.

*It will still give me goosebumps to the day I die. Just incredible, very, very special and an occasion I'll never forget.*

So again, if you were there, thank you. And thanks to all the Forest fans throughout my career, too.

I always felt like I had a good connection with the supporters. Hopefully they saw me as someone who worked hard, made the most of what talent he'd got and always gave everything in every game. Win or lose, I felt it inside and I always played with passion.

So without a doubt, the saddest part of my time at the club was leaving it. I bet that's the same for everyone in this book.

Going wasn't my decision - it was made for me. I think everyone realises that now - and they probably did at the time too. I'd never want to leave of my own accord.

But David Platt came in and he wanted to change things. And as every Forest fan knows, he achieved that. Say no more.

He didn't really have any connection with the club or any affinity with it. Needless to say, we didn't see eye-to-eye. How could we? He wanted rid of all us experienced lads who he called the *'old school'*.

What that really meant was myself, Steve Chettle, Ian Woan were in the firing line, literally.

He got rid of all three of us pretty quickly, which was a real shame. I was gutted, really disappointed with it.

I never wanted to leave and like I mentioned, my aim was to play for Forest all the way through.

In the end, after so long at Forest, everything happened really quickly. I had a move lined up to to Hibs in Scotland, but then Colin Cooper rang me from Boro and said Bryan Robson was interested in taking me over there.

To be honest, Middlesbrough's a lot nearer to Barnsley, the money was better and they had a good squad of players, so that's where I went on a free transfer.

After that, I had spells at Fulham, that goalscoring stint at Wednesday (!), then Oldham and finally Chesterfield.

So all in all, I made the best of what I had, I worked hard and had a good career.

But Forest was without doubt the best time for me, not just in football but in life too.

Anyone who knows me knows what the club means to me and when I look back now, the overwhelming feeling is one of just pride at being able to pull on that shirt so many times and represent the club.

As you can hopefully tell, I love recalling those great days by the Trent - words can't really get across how absolutely brilliant they were.

When it was my 50th birthday, Alan Hill got me a photo-montage of my playing days and I've got that in pride of place at home. I've kept all my medals and the shirts I wore on my debuts for my clubs, but other than that, like I mentioned, I've given a lot of things away.

My memories are in my head and that's all I need, really.

And they're absolutely priceless.

So, if you're still with me, I'll go right back to the start . . . why is 13 *not* unlucky for me?

Well, it's simple - June 1987 to July 2000; 13 years when I got to play for a great club, with some incredible players, in front of amazing fans, starting out under the greatest manager the game has ever seen.

*Unlucky? You're kidding - I was the luckiest lad in the world.*

CHAPTER 5

# JASON LEE: DOWN IN WRITING

When I was younger, I kept a diary. I don't know where I got that from, as it was a bit old school even then.

But as a young lad who loved football, I would set myself targets in this diary; *get a trial, get taken on, pro contract, make my debut, first goal, goal targets*, things like that.

At first, it seemed like pie in the sky as I didn't really have much contact with the professional game until I was about 16.

But then, once I started getting trials and having a glimpse of it, I thought: 'Right, I'm going to do everything possible to be as successful as my ability will take me.'

I was just so focused on making it and if I didn't . . . it wouldn't be for lack of trying.

We lived in a council flat and football was a real chance to break out of my environment.

I had choices to make. I could have gone left or right, continued to hang with the wrong crowd.

I like to think I've got a good head on my shoulders, but so have lots of people and God knows where I might have ended up.

I looked at footballers' lives; the cars, the lifestyle, the whole thing, I suppose.

But more than that, I thought that these guys made a living from playing football - and I loved playing football, so it was a win-win.

It might not totally be in my hands, but for the bit that was - the effort, the commitment, the training, the focus - I made a deal with myself that I would keep up my end of the bargain.

And I put that down in writing.

Now, you might not be surprised to hear this, but when I was younger I used to play a bit of basketball.

I was keen on athletics too - I loved the 200m - as well as football obviously, so I was always outdoors doing something physical, being active.

It took a while for me to be spotted on the football scene even though I played at district level and for London and was always keen for a game - I'd play Saturdays and Sundays, sometimes double-headers.

I went to an all-boys school for a couple of years and the Sunday team I played for had quite a few people who went on to have careers in the game; John Goodman, who played for Wimbledon and was an Irish international, Bobby Bowery, who played for Palace.

That patch of London was a really good recruiting ground and I remember Leo Fortune-West replaced me in the Sunday team a little bit after I left, so there were lots of good players around.

A lot of lads who I played with seemed to get getting trials and whatnot but, like I said, I was 16 before I got in at Charlton, which is quite late in contrast to the modern era.

That probably affected my outlook, because I knew I really had to take this one chance I'd been given, so I didn't go in like a normal young player, worried about the people that were already established there.

I went flying into people in training and I wasn't intimidated by anyone. It got to the point where the manager Lennie Lawrence was saying: 'You've got to calm down, son.'

But I was unrepentant: 'No, I'm here to make my mark.'

And if that meant literally, then that was just part of it.

To be fair, Lennie could probably have sacked me several times for some of my antics when I was a scholar; being over-physical with some of the senior pros, mainly.

I just wasn't used to everything that came with being a young lad starting out in the game - all the 'yes, boss' stuff, cleaning boots, cleaning toilets, the bath, the shower. You name it, we cleaned it.

I was like 'hold on a minute - this is like forced labour'.

I was an east London boy and wouldn't go in digs over at Charlton and was too young to drive, so I left my house at seven in the morning and got back at seven at night. I was shattered, but I applied myself and the opportunity drove me on. It definitely wasn't the pay.

I was getting paid £27-a-week in the first-year YTS, £35 in the second year and if I got on the pitch I think I got £100 appearance money - so you can see why I was so desperate to get in the team.

I just couldn't get my head round that YTS money - it was so poor, given everything we had to do.

Of course, now I look back and think 'yeah, maybe it had to be like that back then'. But I sure as hell didn't like it.

I was in good company though, as we played in the South East Counties league around that time with the likes of Kevin Campbell, Andy Cole and Alan Shearer.

Coley wasn't the player he later became, but Kev Campbell was an absolute machine, scoring a ridiculous amount of goals all by himself.

We beat Southampton at The Dell in the FA Youth Cup and Shearer was playing for them, but he wasn't prolific at the time and didn't really stand out. Then at the weekend, he played for the first team and scored a hat-trick against Arsenal - we couldn't believe it! The rest, as they say, is history.

It shows you've got to take your chance when it comes and me and Scott Minto both made our debuts together in the League Cup against Sunderland.

I was only 17 and a sub for the game, but I got on after 20 minutes and loved it. I'd done well with the youth team and then the reserves, which in those days was up against senior pros, in proper stadiums, so that was a real baptism of fire.

I've coached and managed myself now and the development of players at under-23 games these days leaves a lot to be desired.

It's very sanitised and without the real three points to play for, it's hard to recreate the intensity of a senior game. You don't have the old pros nudging you, tugging you or pulling all the tricks of the trade that come with years playing the game.

I don't want to sound like an old fogey (gimme a break!), but back in the day, you'd play in a proper stadium and if the first team was playing away, the reserves would be in the home ground and you'd get some fans turning up to watch. It was just a far better preparation for the 'real thing', I think.

For example, I played at Anfield for Charlton reserves and there was a good crowd on because the first team was away and that type of experience really helped bring players on.

You even got your first taste of Scouse 'wit' (I use the term loosely there) with the odd heckle from the terraces.

I was in and around the team at Charlton but getting frustrated really, as I was always impatient to progress and Lennie made me wait until I was 18 for my first pro contract, even though I'd played in the first team at 17. I was like: 'Aww c'mon man! What's the hold-up? Have you seen the YTS money?'

When I eventually did sign, it was only a 12-month deal for about £100-a-week, maybe £150 with incentives, which doesn't sound like a lot now, but you had to earn it.

Joking aside, the money wasn't really that important, the real value was the opportunity I was being given.

One day, I saw Lennie talking to this chap on the training ground and the pair of them came over to talk to me.

The fella was the manager of nearby non-league side Fisher Athletic - the great Malcolm Allison.

To be honest, being a young lad, I didn't really know as much as I should have done about him, but Fisher were in the Conference at the time and he asked if I fancied going on loan for a month.

Like a lot of young players, I didn't really want to drop down to non-league at that stage but at the end of the day, I needed games and to play men's football.

On top of that, one or two people took me aside and said: 'Look, this is Malcolm Allison, you can learn a hell of a lot from him . . .'

So that's what I did and I absolutely loved it; I played games, scored goals, it really helped my game and Malcolm was fantastic, such a knowledgeable football guy and as a character - well, it was Malcolm Allison.

If you're reading this and you're old enough, you'll know what I mean. If not, look him up, because he was a real football pioneer.

But I'd caught his eye and I always remember being told that I had a real shot at making a career if I gave everything every time I went out to play.

Even years later, coaches and managers would tell me they'd seen me play in this game or that game and I think that's why I never struggled to get a club throughout my career.

You never know who's watching and you know they're seeing what your attitude is like, as much as your ability.

People had seen that I always gave everything, every time I went on the pitch.

When I came back from Fisher I went out on another loan, up to Stockport this time, which was harder for me, as I was a London boy and had really only left the city on a coach.

I remember driving up there and it just seemed to take forever - seven or eight hours, the weather was horrendous and I was thinking: 'It's like the end of the world up here!'

I had to go into digs, which I didn't like, and the month was a complete wash-out.

(I know, rain in Manchester, who'd have thought it, eh?)

I scored a hat-trick in a behind-closed-doors game though and Stockport were the biggest team physically I'd ever played in - probably including some of my old basketball teams.

Danny Bergara was the manager there - another real character and a former Uruguayan international, so you might not expect his teams to have been so, err, direct.

But to give you an idea, I played up front with Kevin Francis, who was 6ft 7ins and basically, if you were below 6ft 4ins, you looked out of place.

One of the games I did manage to play was against Lincoln, who were managed by Steve Thompson, a former Charlton team-mate and during the game he was talking to me, saying: 'You're signing for us next week, Jason.'

It was a bit bizarre, but good news all the same, as I definitely preferred signing for Lincoln over staying underwater in Stockport.

A few days later, I was in Danny's office and he was calling Charlton trying to do a deal to sign me when he found out I was going to Lincoln.

I was only young so I was sat there trying to look all innocent and a bit sheepish about it, but Danny was taking no prisoners. He put the phone down went absolutely off on one, shouting: 'Get out of my office and don't come back! Go on - get out!'

My Uruguayan isn't great, but I don't think he was wishing me all the best.

It's funny to look back on it now, but at the time I just dived for the door and was like: 'Wow! That's crazy!'

Funnily enough, we were up against the clock so we had to do the deal at Sheffield United and Dave Bassett was there - it's funny how paths cross in football.

Lincoln had paid £35,000 for me, which was hardly a fortune but back then for a young player going to the Fourth Division it was a decent sum and Lennie made sure there was a sell-on clause, so he was a sharp operator.

I think I should probably have played more for Charlton. I look back and a mate of mine, Carl Leaburn, was there and he played for them for years.

To be honest, I never thought they developed his game as much as they could have done to get the very best out of Carl, so maybe it's a case of 'be careful what you wish for'.

I could have played quite a lot for Charlton, but not been able to improve my game half as much as I did by going out and playing different styles, particularly in Nottingham.

For me, going out was a chance to prove myself and it was only a couple of years later that I was battering Lennie's Middlesbrough team with Forest.

When I got to Lincoln, one of the things that happened was that I was away from my favourite barber in London, so I started to let my hair grow longer. Obviously, I didn't realise that would be such a big thing in the years to come for reasons beyond my control.

I played regularly for Lincoln and that was the most important thing for me - to play games.

Unfortunately, my disciplinary record there was shocking. At one point I'm sure it was the worst in the country; I was getting booked and sent off way too often.

Part of it was my physical approach, but a big part of it was what went on behind the ref's back; the spitting, punching, kicking, ankle-tapping, it was unbelievable.

Throw in plenty of casual racism and it was a real testing ground. I could cope with the physicality, but the abuse and the mental side of it was a massive challenge too.

Centre-halves would always be trying to leave a mark, get at you, smash you to the floor, and I had to fight fire with fire - it was sink or swim.

Look, I'm a London boy so that side of it never fazed me. I was never going to back down but I realised what they were trying to do;

get in my head, get me booked or sent off. So I learned to play the game and channel aggression properly - over time, of course, and that's why that experience is so valuable.

I remember we played Forest in a behind-closed-doors game not long after they signed Stan Collymore and Colin Cooper and I remember giving Coops and Steve Chettle a real battering.

Soon after that, I went to Southend to replace Stan and then within that same season, I was off again to join Forest.

At the time, I saw Southend as the next Wimbledon. Barry Fry was there and had brought half the Barnet squad with him - some really good players.

He'd spent the money from Stan's transfer well, bringing me in from Lincoln and Ricky Otto in from Leyton Orient. Jamie Lawrence was on trial, so that could have been a great front three - if only for the hairstyles back then.

We drew with Forest 1-1 on the opening day of the season, which was a good result, but I can tell you now that EVERY team in the league wanted to beat Forest that year.

They were this massive club who had won the European Cup and were now playing the likes of Southend.

Not that I played that day though; I was suspended after getting sent off (yes, again) for Lincoln the previous year.

I didn't actually tell Barry Fry about missing the first three games of the season until AFTER I'd signed the contract. When I did drop the bad news in to him, I got the full Barry-effin-Fry effect for the next five minutes: 'Youuuu're effin' whaaat, son?!!!'

When he calmed down, some of the results we got were incredible; we drew with Forest, beat Wolves away, beat Sunderland away, Derby away and by Christmas we were up to third in the table. Southend pushing for the Prem!

At which point, I think the club panicked when the realisation of potentially being in the Premier League hit home off the pitch; all the contracts would have to be looked at, the ground would need upgrading. All sorts of things started to be flagged up.

Personally, I thought we could have done a Wimbledon and survived despite the small crowds, but I don't think the club was ready for it - Barry left for Birmingham and the team got broken up, which was really sad at the time.

Forest were right up at the top of the league that season, but with the run-in looming, they'd had a bit of an injury crisis. Stan was injured and Robert Rosario was out too. Gary Bull, a great little player from Barnet, was there but was struggling a bit. Lee Glover was there, but again, he was a different type of player to Stan and Robert.

Frank himself was a very impressive guy; charismatic, friendly, and clued up about any player you'd mention to him.

He was very intelligent and I think he had had gone into the City Ground with the aim of changing the culture and shaking things up a bit.

Having gone down the year before, he wanted more physical power, more hunger and to take a more modern approach to things behind the scenes.

I also think Frank had seen me battering Chetts and Coops when Southend had played Forest that season and liked the look of me.

So when this injury crisis kicked in with about 15 games left, it was a good move for everyone for me to go to Nottingham - and believe me I was absolutely buzzing to be there.

I met Frank and Alan Hill, another great guy, and I was lucky enough to play towards the rest of that 93/94 season when we got promoted back to the Premier League.

There were some big - no, HUGE - characters in that dressing room but I wasn't intimidated and, again, I think that was the key to settling in quickly.

I had massive respect for these players, but Frank also brought in people who really needed to make their mark; people like Des Lyttle, as well as some outstanding foreign lads like Lars Bohinen and Alf-Inge Haaland.

Maybe when he'd got there, there were one or two established players who had lost that need to prove themselves.

The new people coming in saw a move to Forest as an incredible opportunity and, for me, it was a chance I wasn't going to let get away.

If there was a running session, I was always up near the front because I wanted to do it - I had that drive and I wanted to be noticed.

They hadn't paid a massive fee for me - it was around £200,000 - but I didn't go there to be a makeshift centre-forward, to be Stan's temporary stand-in, I went to earn a place in the side and then keep it.

If I'm being critical, from the outside perhaps the previous Forest squad had had a bit of a soft underbelly, where they weren't as strong physically or mentally as they needed to be to stay up the year before.

Obviously, that didn't apply to Stuart Pearce (!) but overall, you can see why Frank bought the type of players he did, to show that Forest would no longer be a team that could play football on their day, but were also a bit of a soft touch if you got at them.

When I went into that dressing room, my attitude hadn't changed since Day One in South London. I wasn't fazed and I wanted to play - it was as simple as that.

I remember the first time I turned up, I was driving this blue Wrangler Jeep; huge wheels, fold-down windscreen, big sound system, the lot. A proper footballer's motor . . !

It should have been patrolling Jurassic park, but here's me driving it round Nottingham like the king of the world.

I pulled onto the City Ground car park packed with these nice shiny, very 'grown up' BMWs and I was like: 'Okaaay.'

I had this - how can I put it? - 'edgy' look and I jump out with my dreadlocks, go in the dressing room and the first thing I did was head for the tape-deck, take out whatever was playing and start banging out some drum'n'bass at full pelt.

That was my introduction to the team and, of course, Pearcey's in the corner with a right look on his face going: 'Ere . . . now hold on a minute son!'

The lads loved it though and it was a great initiation for me - and them. If nothing else, I'll improve the music round here.

Very quickly, I could see how Frank had got the dressing room just right; he'd got a really good collection of players all with the right attitude and desire to do well.

I just wasn't dazzled by reputations and if you want to succeed, that's the best way to be.

When I did play, no-one was going to push me around and I'd give every last drop of everything I had for the team.

That was how I looked at every game. Of course, some days are better than others. Sometimes things come off and others they don't. Sometimes the guy marking you just gets the better of you - it happens to everyone.

But no matter what, my attitude was always the same - just give everything. If you do that, people will remember it - and you can hold your head up high.

My first goal came a few weeks after I signed, against Middlesboro and my old boss Lennie Lawrence.

Frank played me and Robert Rosario that day, which he didn't normally do. I think in all honesty, I'd been brought in to replace Robert, who was the wrong side of 30 by then and hadn't scored that many goals.

Stan was still recovering from injury and both Robert and me scored that night.

Kingsley Black put a great cross in and I got a good header in in front of Alan Kernaghan to score, so it was great to get one over Len. (Make me wait til I'm 18 for a contract, will you boss? Right - payback.)

Joking aside, he's a great guy and many years later of course, he came to the City Ground with Dougie Freedman and we'd always laugh about that goal up at the Riverside. Well . . . I'd laugh!

The following week, I finally got to play at The Valley when we took on Charlton. When I was starting out, we'd been ground-sharing with Crystal Palace, so to go there, Portakabins and all, and see the stadium back in action was just fantastic.

Then to get the winner . . . well, you couldn't write that script and it was a real moment for me; left foot, through the keeper's legs. I can still see it now.

I'd actually scored for Southend against them earlier that season so to do it twice was fantastic - not out of anything other than showing them that I could play at that level and what they'd missed out on.

But you have to move on and my focus was purely Forest.

For us to go back up at the first attempt wasn't easy, because like I mentioned, we were a real scalp in that division and there were some big clubs chasing us; Wolves, Sunderland . . . Derby.

*Did I say big clubs? I mean some big clubs and some medium-sized ones (!).*

I think the game everyone remembers from that run-in was Peterborough away and I definitely hadn't seen anything like it up to that point in my career.

The Forest fans were everywhere you looked - I'm pretty sure there were more locked out as well that day, because there just seemed to be these red shirts all over the place.

Peterborough were rock bottom of the league, already relegated and I think people maybe saw it as a foregone conclusion that we would win.

But I tell you what, they still had some good players and football, well . . . it can trip you up at any point.

Seven minutes in and we were 2-0 down. Disaster.

Thankfully Stan got one back before half-time and Pearcey dived through a mass of flying boots to bring us level.

I'd come on as a sub and managed to chest a long goal kick from Mark Crossley into the path of Steve Stone, who fed Stan and well, Stan did what Stan does, an absolute screamer into the top corner to seal promotion. The scenes . . !

We could probably have done without the drama, but looking back, what a day that was.

The celebrations were long, hard and fully deserved that season and it was just brilliant for me to play a part in getting Forest back to where they should be in the Premier League.

That summer, the pre-season training was hard but brilliant and a real eye-opener. Frank had brought in a fitness coach who he'd worked with before and we were doing all sorts of things that were innovative at the time, working with parachutes - running with them, not jumping out of planes! - and just generally moving the dial as to what the routine had previously been like at the club.

And I'm telling you now . . . it was hard.

I'm not calling anyone out, but there were some players who did not enjoy those sessions at the time. There was a lot of tired legs, tired arms, tired everything.

I never minded it, but Stan didn't enjoy it - he just came to life during games.

A shooting session or a practice match, he'd be up for it, but any Monday to Friday slog wasn't really his thing.

The other thing Frank had tackled was the drinking culture, which existed at many clubs back then.

I was teetotal when I played, I wanted to give myself the best chance to succeed and I just don't think you can recover quickly enough when you're a professional athlete and games are coming thick and fast.

On Monday mornings, some players would be shocking in training and it might take days for them to get to the level they needed to be.

I think Frank brought in a new professionalism and recruited some good people around him.

The previous era had been great in its day but now there needed to be a change in the philosophy and the outlook of the club and I think most people recognised that.

Pre-match, I always needed to eat fairly early and again, it would be the classic, bland pre-football meal; chicken, pasta. It wasn't great, but nutritionally it was what was required.

At the end of it all though, there was no way anyone could accuse that squad of having a soft underbelly.

We barely had a belly between us! We were so, so fit - and I'd always been naturally fit and strong. But this was something else.

And it gave us that belief that we were ready for the Premiership, as it was back then.

Mentally, we had no fear.

The club didn't have a fortune to spend, but the gaffer went for quality over quantity and brought in Bryan Roy - a great lad and a top, top player.

When he first came in, he spoke very little English, but he had this glint in his eye and that little look. That big smile was often all you needed to know what he was thinking.

Obviously, he'd just played in the World Cup, so he brought that little bit of star quality, but he fitted in with the group straight away.

At first teams would try to bully him, but he had such quick feet, he'd just bounce back up and get on with it and that used to frustrate opponents - they could see this guy wasn't backing down.

Certainly in that first season he had that approach, maybe he got tired of the physical side in his second and third years and lost a bit of that desire, but in Year One with Stan he formed a great partnership and showed his class on a weekly basis.

I know players, especially top players, can be temperamental and want to play in certain positions, so maybe that knocked Bryan off course a bit later in his time at Forest, but nothing should take away how good he was in that first year.

We were quite revolutionary back then, in that we played with a Number 10, five midfielders and one striker, a lot of the time under Frank.

If you're that one striker, whether it be me, Stan or Bryan, you need to occupy two centre halves and look after the ball.

It wasn't easy and no striker really enjoys playing up there all on your own. Stan was great at it, because he could pick the ball up anywhere and run past players.

But generally, if you're up there on your own, you're relying on midfielders to get up with you or go past you and that's what we had in that team.

Lars Bohinen, Scot Gemmill, Stevie Stone, Ian Woan, Chris Bart-Williams - all these guys were capable of doing that and we were so fortunate to have them all around that time.

The other thing was, Pearcey was getting double figures every season from left back, Coops would always chip in, so there were goals throughout that team.

This was the era when there were only two substitutions allowed from the bench so a lot of the time that season, I was coming on and trying to make an impact in games.

The team was doing well, so it was a case of busting a gut not only to maintain standards but also to maybe dislodge Bryan or Stan, which was never going to be easy that year.

I had a good spell when I came on and scored three in five matches, away at Newcastle, home to Spurs and then away again at Leicester where we won.

So I was getting a bit of a 'Supersub' tag which no-one really wants, to be honest!

But the manager knew that if he did put me on, I could impact a game and my attitude would be spot on.

I wanted to play, but I wasn't one to whinge or moan if I wasn't starting every week. I'd just get out there, give it everything I'd got and I don't think centre halves would have looked forward to me coming on, especially late when they might be looking to see games out.

I'd get on there and be like: 'Nah! You're going to have to work for this mate!'

The only one I really missed out on was the 7-1 win away at Sheffield Wednesday, which was an amazing performance by the lads.

Des Walker was playing for Wednesday and he had so much talent, it's hard to feel sorry for him, but as the goals went in and the Forest fans gave it the old 'you'll never beat Des Walker' chant . . . my heart went out to him. Well, a little bit.

I made some starts that season alongside both Bryan and Stan and I think we did well together whoever was starting.

Obviously, Stan and I are very different players - I played the traditional Number 9 role; heading the ball, holding it up, doing all the ugly stuff that Stan didn't really enjoy.

So if I played alongside him, I had to look on him as a smaller centre forward, even though he was quite a big lad. I'd be looking for him to run in behind, go short, pull out slightly wide, while I had to be disciplined and occupy the centre halves.

Sometimes you need that pivotal player in the team - holding a position and letting the others know where there was always an outlet - and I was happy for it to be me.

Looking back over the season, the team had done brilliantly, finishing third in the Premiership and I thought I'd made the transition to the top tier well.

Less than 18 months earlier, I'd been at Lincoln, so the rise had been quick, but I think I earned it.

I hadn't really had the chance to play at Charlton, so I'd taken a gamble to drop down the leagues, to get games and experience and now it had paid off.

I knew I could play at a high level and when I got my opportunity I just thought: 'Yeah, I can do this.'

There was a lot of hype around certain players in the Premiership and a lot of talk about hard men and whatnot. But when I played against them, I thought: 'Really? Is that it?'

They didn't live up to it for me. From where I'd come from, not just London, but from the bottom division, no-one wanted it more than me.

Gary Pallister was different class in terms of defending, but I felt more comfortable with the physicality in the Premiership than at the lower levels, where you could get in some right altercations.

What I hadn't been used to was that level of exposure.

Now, I'd already played long enough to know you were always going to get stick at away grounds, no matter who you were, no matter where you played - the fans were going to be on at you.

But with me, I had another level to cope with - Fantasy Football.

The show went out on a Friday evening and was fresh in people's minds on the Saturday and yes, it was a different time, a different era.

They'd take the Mickey out of all sorts of people - even Pele, so I suppose I was in good company there. And, yes, I understood the humour of it to a degree, but it went too far.

Probably because of the stick I'd taken in games I was a bit more hardened to it.

It was my family and friends who got wound up by it more than me. But the 'black-facing' and the overtones . . . looking back, it went too far.

When you're out there playing, you can always block it out or shut people up by scoring a goal.

I'd get it at every away ground, but it just made me more determined and when I scored a goal I was like: 'Who's laughing now then?'

One of the reasons I didn't get my hair cut was because I was so stubborn, I didn't want to look like I was giving in to bullies. I work in equalities now with the PFA and I think the game understands that type of bullying more now and knows how to tackle it, but at the time, I just had to get on with it.

I'm lucky in that I had broad shoulders, especially as I was still quite young at the time, 23 or something like that and maybe the show should have let it go. Me and Des Lyttle used to watch it before away games and I think they milked it for longer than it was funny. Come on, have you not got any new material?

I wanted to be judged on playing my football and that whole Fantasy Football thing got blurred between appearance, race and things that took it away from football.

I always get asked about it and it'll probably be with me to my dying day, but I always try to turn these things into a positive, so I talk to young players now about how to handle things like that.

Because there's no doubt you can go under if you haven't got that mental toughness or support around you.

Me? I was NEVER going to go under. There's far, far worse things out there and at the end of the day, I was being paid to play football for a great club in the Premiership, so I was doing OK, y'know?

I'd worked hard to get to where I was and a bit of stick on the TV wasn't going to make me give it all up. As if.

It's like: 'Say what you like mate, but I'm playing up front for Nottingham Forest in the Premier League on Saturday. What are you doing?'

Funnily enough, towards the end of my time at Forest, we played away at Chelsea, where David Baddiel has a season ticket and I was on the bench.

I'd had my hair cut by then, not because of any stick, but just because I wanted to move on and change my style, but they were still giving me grief every time I went to warm up.

I was desperate to get on and kept badgering Frank: 'Just get me on the park gaffer - let me leave my mark on these guys!'

I remember my brother and my nephew were there and I was absolutely straining to get out there and do something.

Luckily, I got the shout to replace Bryan at half-time.

We were 1-0 down but I absolutely ran myself into the ground, I was so fired up - even more than usual.

Right at the end, the 90th minute, I chased a long ball into the box, caught it on the half volley and - bang - it clipped the post before dropping in.

I can see it now. Stamford Bridge, 40,000 on . . . and you could have heard a pin drop.

Best feeling in the world. That's what you're there for and believe me, that was a special celebration. You beauty.

Football gives you an opportunity to prove people wrong and you've just got to take it. Thanks very much.

As we approached the 1995/96 season though, we faced up to life without Stan after he left for Liverpool.

The club moved fast with the tried and tested Kev Campbell coming in as well as the Italian Andrea Silenzi who was a bit more of an unknown quality.

I liked Andy, he was a great lad. Part of the deal was for us to play Torino in a pre-season friendly and he looked after us. Me, Des Lyttle and Chris Bart Williams went shopping with him and there we were in Turin round all these fancy Italian shops - a different world.

Look, everyone knows what happened with Andrea at Forest.

His record was great; he captained Torino, he played with Diego Maradona, he'd played for Italy . . . technically, he was very, very good.

But this was the English Premier League and even though he was a big lad - it was very different to what he'd been used to.

In training, with a bit more time and space, he'd score these incredible goals and things and I remember the looks on some of the lads' faces thinking: 'Yeah right, mate. Try that on a Saturday and see how far it gets you.'

Because you just wouldn't get the chance to do that with a Premier League centre half kicking you three feet up in the air.

And I think that's what he struggled to come to terms with.

He was the first Italian in the Premier League, didn't speak much English and it couldn't have been easy for him.

Everyone knows it didn't work out, but I think it would be different these days as clubs have liaison officers and are a lot more in tune with helping new signings adjust.

I think at the time, it was a case of: 'Here's Nottingham - enjoy!'

So I have a bit of sympathy for him.

Obviously Kev was a lot more used to the physicality of the league and things were going well.

We went 12 games unbeaten at the start of that season and I got six goals over that spell.

Everything was looking good until we went to Blackburn in early October.

I'd started the game up front on my own and early the second half I got put through on goal, one-on-one with Tim Flowers.

He charged out and absolutely mullered me with his knee, right in the quad. Oh my life, the pain! The worst dead leg I've ever had. Normally you can run them off, but this was straight through to the bone and I couldn't even get up. I still give Tim stick about it to this day.

I was stretchered off and then about 15 minutes later Stevie Chettle got sent off - and that was it . . . the floodgates opened.

I remember lying on the treatment table under their main stand and just kept hearing these cheers thinking: 'Blimey - not another one!'

Lars Bohinen had just gone there for a decent fee from Forest and he got two that day, Shearer got a hat-trick and it ended up 7-0. (SEVEN-nil as the old TV vidiprinter used to say, just to RUB IT IN.)

So that was a painful trip north in every sense and now we knew what Sheff Wednesday must have felt like.

When that happens, the coach journey back is painful, I can tell you. Fans may be fed up, but trust me, the players are too and it's just absolutely miserable. Any defeat is bad, but 7-0? Totally depressing.

It was out of character for us that year though, because by then not only had we started the Premiership campaign well - we'd kicked off our UEFA Cup campaign too.

I loved those European nights and the atmosphere at the City Ground in those games was off the scale.

Bryan grabbed an absolute screamer to put us through against Malmo and the noise that night was just incredible. I think it took the fans back to the Brian Clough era of those great European nights. They were such great things to be part of and it was special to be out there. You could feel the passion and the drive of the fans for European glory.

It sounds cheesy and it's hard to describe, but I'm telling you . . . there was a special push from the City Ground on those nights.

A lot of English teams had gone out early on and for unfancied Forest to be flying the flag that year was a great feeling - we genuinely thought we could go all the way because we had no fear at all.

I led the line against Auxerre, where they had some great players including Laurent Blanc, Taribo West and one Sabri Lamouchi. There's a great picture of me holding his head in the palm of my hand in a little skirmish which I've reminded him of in recent times and we've had a laugh about it.

Who would have thought that one day their midfield dynamo would end up managing Forest?

But we got through those games and Paul McGregor's goal put us through against Lyon over two legs.

I've got to be honest, I was disappointed not to start the Bayern game in Munich, but Frank went with Kev and we got a good result out there thanks to Chetts.

In the home leg, well, I came on and got an assist for Steve Stone's goal, but once they got the away goal at the City Ground it was always going to be a tough night. What a team they had though - absolutely frightening and if we had to go out, at least it was to the eventual winners.

But for me personally, I remember that season well; I played a lot of games, led the line and joint top scored with Bryan.

Frank had brought in other players, so the competition was there in the squad, but I held my own and we were still a good team, finishing eighth. Of course, we were going to miss Stan's goals but I think we did well and there was nothing to suggest the wheels were going to fall off the following year.

I missed the first game of the season when Kev got a hat-trick and we beat Coventry 3-0 at their place but after that, everything just seemed to go wrong.

There were glimpses of what we could do - we went 1-0 up at Manchester United, but ended up getting beat 4-1 and it was just a really frustrating time.

Dean Saunders had come in to give us more experience up top, but for whatever reason, we were struggling for goals.

I was coming off the bench more than starting games but to be fair to Frank, he was just trying to find a solution to our losing run.

Maybe expectation got to the club because I think the team had over-achieved in the previous couple of years, but the decision to sack Frank in December of that season was crazy in my view.

It's not as if the club had spent ridiculous amounts of money and you would have thought that everything Frank achieved would have counted for something.

Unfortunately, when we had a dip, it clearly didn't.

I just thought, well, there's no loyalty in the game.

If Frank had have stayed, I'm confident we could have stayed up and built again from there the following season.

Obviously, Pearcey took over and did well at first but with no management experience, taking over a situation like that was a hell of a thing.

It wasn't easy for Stuart, going from playing to management out of the blue and, in short, it all went pear-shaped.

The atmosphere wasn't the same, the dressing room was demoralised and there was a lack of heart. If you do that to a dressing room, it's only going to end one way.

It wasn't Stuart or Dave Bassett's fault, but things changed when Frank went and it felt like a different club.

I could sense my time was coming to an end and went out on loan to Charlton and Grimsby in the second half of that season, but I came back just as relegation was being confirmed and it was just horrible.

I was on the bench a couple of times and I just didn't want to get on, it was that bad.

I knew my time was up and I was being shown the door.

Pierre van Hooijdonk had come in and I wasn't part of it any more. That's why I'd gone out on loan, to get some games. I'd only started half a dozen or so all season and I'm not daft - when it gets like that, the writing is on the wall.

Dave Bassett had made changes and had hung his hat on Pierre, so I wasn't going to get a look-in really, even though I was probably his type of player.

In the end, I slipped out quietly for roughly the same fee as when I'd signed.

Graham Taylor was at Watford and had been watching me, even though they were in League 1 at the time.

I think Forest got a fee very similar to the one they'd paid out to Southend so it was a good deal all round and I think looking back, I gave good service to the club.

We had a successful promotion campaign at Watford and that was good for my soul after the way things had ended at Forest.

I've got four children and my family was settled in the area, so I tried to stay around the Nottingham area for the rest of my career really - it's a beautiful city and the people are really friendly.

I played for a lot of clubs and if I'd have uprooted my family every time I moved, you can imagine the upheaval that would have caused.

I talk to players about it now. A new manager can come in and not fancy you as a player and it doesn't matter if you've just moved house, got your family settled, got the kids in a new school - they're not bothered. That's the brutal reality of football and you've got to protect your family from things like that.

Luckily, I ended up back on my doorstep at Notts County at the age of 35, playing for my old Lincoln boss Steve Thompson again. I was captain and got 16 goals in my first season - as well as 18 bookings.

Steve was joking saying: 'Yep, you haven't changed a bit!'

But it wasn't me. It was the game changing.

A lot of my bookings were for people feigning injury. It was embarrassing. You'd look at people rolling around on the floor and think: 'Really?'

I played for Mansfield and Kettering later on and I was 38 when I finished playing, so never struggled for a contract in a 20-year career in the game. After that, I coached at Notts County and Forest, as well as having a spell as manager at Boston United. These days, I'm happy and kept busy with my equalities work at the PFA.

Overall, I enjoyed playing for all my clubs, for different reasons each time. At Forest, it was everything I wanted it to be - and more.

Hopefully they'd say the same about me.

I don't think when I went in for a relatively small fee that people would have expected much from me.

Stan was the big money signing - he had the expectation and he lived up to that.

Me? I went there for a lot less; played a lot of games, scored goals, led the line, put my body out there, kept some other big money son the bench and gave everything for the shirt every single game I played.

I wasn't getting anywhere near the money of some of the people I was keeping out of the team at times, but it didn't matter to me - I just wanted to play, to show what I could do and be the best I could be.

I've kept my links with the club over the years; I work in education with them, do some ambassadorial work and sit on the community trust board - it's a great club with good people, both inside and out.

It will always be a big part of my life and I wouldn't have it any other way.

The memories I have are priceless and my most important contract was the one I made with myself when I was starting out: 'Give it everything you've got - and see where it takes you.'

*I've probably still got that written down in a diary somewhere.*

CHAPTER 6

# BRYAN ROY: CALL ME BRYAN

We didn't have a lot when I was growing up as a kid in Amsterdam. I didn't have loads of toys and this was the days before Xbox and things. But I did have a ball - and I used to drive my mum crazy with it.

Imagine me, with a ball - indoors. *Kick, kick, kick*, all day.

It wasn't even a full-sized football, but I was always kicking it around the house, making a mess, breaking things. Maybe that's why I learned to control it so well - there would have been no ornaments left standing!

Anyway, this small ball was great, because it made your touch better and eventually - *finally!* - when I got a full-sized ball, well, it seemed easier to control than this little thing I'd been using.

Whenever I kicked a bigger ball, it was easier for me after trying all day with this small thing.

So, eventually she got me a bright orange FULL-SIZED ball. What a day!

Simple things, simple pleasures.

This one was too big for the house, so no more damage. I had to get outside where I'd find a patch of grass - more often mud or concrete - and a wall and I'd just kick this ball up against it, day in, day out or play with anyone I could find.

We'd have these big games, no referees of course - come on! Who wants to be a referee? We wanted to PLAY.

It was a very happy childhood. I used to live just over the road from my school and there was a big square just next door, so we always had space to kick about.

We were in a flat on the fourth floor but I didn't mind that either - it made my legs stronger. Up and down, up and down.

That's the way I looked at it, all those stairs were helping me. No problem.

I played in a couple of youth teams there which were at a good standard and I was spotted by Ajax where Johan Cruyff was running things.

What a guy. He would always encourage you to be brave on the ball - which I suppose was a lot easier if you were Johan Cruyff!

But for us young players, we liked that too. No fear, you know? Express yourselves, show what you can do. Don't be afraid to try things.

Cruyff played this attacking 3-4-3 formation and it rewarded you if you were brave, so there was no pain if you tried something and it didn't come off. It was a case of learning the game but also what you were capable of - if you didn't try it, how would you know?

It was always 'play forward, look forward, pass forward' - always offensive. Looking to get at the opposition. A great outlook.

For me, the De Boers, Denis Bergkamp, we were just having so much fun together in those teams growing up. That's how I remember it - fun.

It wasn't like we were looking to break into the first team the next day or the next week - that would happen when it happened.

For us, we were learning, we were playing and we were having fun. It was a great education and you can see why that Ajax system became the one that everybody in the world looked at. How are they doing it? They came and they learned too.

I was still quite young when I made it into the first team there and it all just seemed like a natural progression. I didn't think 'oh wow, what am I doing here?' I was more like 'well this is the next step, let's enjoy it and see where it goes'.

Of course, I was nervous but more than that, I was excited. You've got to use those nerves in the right way.

Luckily, Ajax was a great team and when I made my debut in 1987 I managed to score as we won 6-1.

I was just 17. It seems like yesterday, but it was so long ago.

We were successful as a team and won the UEFA Cup in 1992 and I absolutely loved it. Playing with some top, top guys; Wim Jonk, Danny Blind - great, great players.

I was in the Dutch squad for the 1990 World Cup and '92 European Championships and loved playing alongside Ruud Gullit and Marco Van Basten - truly, great players of the modern game.

And at home, I was playing for Ajax so I was living the dream as a young man in his early twenties, although eventually I fell out with the coach there - Louis Van Gaal - over football reasons, purely football.

It wasn't money or anything like that. But it was probably down to negative emotions on my side. I didn't have to leave and maybe I should have stayed, but I take responsibility for it and it opened the door to new adventures for me.

Ajax won the Champions League a couple of years later and I was pleased for the club and the guys. But, yes, I look back at times and think 'did I make the right move to go to Foggia?' And if you have those doubts, then I suppose it is never good.

My agent at the time was Mini Raiola who has gone on to be a so-called super agent looking after the likes of Paul Pogba and Zlatan.

But for me, we were both young, starting out and he was a friend. He came out to stay with me in Italy to make sure I settled in.

We were both at the start of adventures and he helped out with all sorts of things, even helping paint my apartment - so you can see he was more than an agent.

I'm not sure he does that for players these days - hey, I'm pretty sure he doesn't need to!

I found the Italian league quite tough, to be honest. It was more physical than I was used to and more defensive, less space.

People who think it might be slow are wrong, those games are fast and they go fast. You have to be on it in Italy all the time, because those defenders are on you straight away. It was good for my game to learn to cope with that and definitely helped me when I came to Forest. Think quick Bryan, y'know!

We did well and came very, very close to qualifying for Europe which for Foggia, would have been amazing. It was a good club with a really forward-thinking coach called Zdenek Zeman, who loved attacking football. Even now, there's a term for it in Italy Zemanlandia, that people still use.

Inevitably, he got noticed by bigger clubs and left for Lazio and I thought maybe it was time for a change.

The move to England came about almost out of the blue - the new manager told me there had been an approach and asked if I would like to talk to Forest.

This was just before the World Cup in 1994 and it was good for me that they were so keen to sign me before the tournament. It gave me that confidence that they wanted me no matter how I played in the USA, where I did OK, but I wasn't really happy with my performances.

They were OK. I preferred the European Championship in 1992 where we reached the semi-final. That was a better tournament for me.

The deal got done while I was in the USA really - I think Frank Clark flew all the way over to see me, but I missed him. I hope he got a tan while he was there!

When it was all sorted, well, I knew about the English Premier League, which was just starting to take off, but also I knew about Nottingham Forest.

When I was younger I'd had the old Panini stickers and this one always caught my eye; it was the Forest badge. It is like no other badge or logo I'd ever seen and when I got this sticker, I kept hold of it and treasured it.

When Forest won the European Cup twice I was thinking: 'These guys must be huge in England. They have Trevor Francis! They've won the European Cup. What a team.'

I'd pictured them in my mind and could see the shirt and the stadium, so when I heard they wanted to sign me, it was like everything was meant to be.

When I arrived in England, Alan Hill collected me from the airport and made me feel so welcome. He was so friendly and so warm as a person. It was like we were friends straight away. In Italy, maybe you were always a player - here you were a person. You could see straight away, the club cared about you and you were straight away part of the family. I liked that. It was a big thing.

Later on I found out that Mino had wanted me to stay in Italy, maybe with Inter Milan, who were asking about me. Maybe Parma or Napoli, I don't know.

But I was happy with my choice, even though Forest had only just got back in the Premier League.

Right at the end, Arsenal were asking, but I had already given my word to Forest and that was that. I wouldn't let anyone down and I'd already got a good feeling about this move.

I can't explain it but deep down, I felt at home. Nottingham was a different city than what I'd been used to, for sure, but I liked it. I liked the fact you could be in the city and then five minutes later, wide open country. Beautiful scenery. I had a wife and young baby and wanted quiet, so no problem with Nottingham at all.

Later on, I said something stupid about how it was dull and all about Robin Hood, but that was just me being stupid, joking about, saying something throwaway and I wish I'd never said it.

I took it back as soon as I said it because it's just . . . balls!

People who know me know I say crazy things sometimes, but trust me I was happy there and still enjoy going back.

The people were so, so friendly. I loved being out and about with them and I tried to pick up the language as fast as I could. We studied English at school, so it wasn't completely new to me and I think I picked it up quite quickly. 'Man on!' The important stuff, y'know?

I don't know about the accent though - I think I still sound Dutch.

*'Men on!'*

'What, two guys Bryan?'

*'No, no, just one!'*

But we got there on the pitch and the guys helped me a lot.

Most importantly, I could understand Frank Clark - maybe better than some of the English guys could because he has this big accent, yes? But to me, English was English, so no problem.

He made a really good impression on me - such a gentleman and someone who had achieved so much in the game. Straight-talking and a top coach.

One of the first things he did was ask me if I wanted to play on the left side or just behind Stan Collymore and at that point I knew enough.

For a coach to be asking me where I thought I'd play best was so meaningful to me. He was a coach who would listen to my opinion and play to my strengths.

I could play in a number of positions up front and we would talk about where best that would be at times, but mainly at that point, I preferred to play down the middle - the partnership with Stan was the best for me.

I'd heard of him before, but when I saw him up close, I was like 'Wow! Yes, I think I can play with this guy!'

Really, it was looking at it and seeing how I could serve the team best. You wanted to do that for the club, for your teammates and for Frank, because he treated you with so much respect.

I felt that if I said something, he would hear it. That's not the case with every coach.

Of course, you have to show the coach it can work and I scored against Olympiakos in a friendly, then again pre-season against Orient, so I think Frank had confidence about the move to the middle.

When I had my signing photo on the pitch, they got me with a Forest scarf, a ball - and an American flag!

I said: 'Hold on! Where's the Dutch flag?'

But I was just joking - this was a really big point of my career. I'd always watched English football on TV but now I was HERE. Don't get me wrong, I had sometimes thought it was behind the times, but it had improved quickly over that period.

The Premier League was new and for sure, the money was good, but it wasn't the fortunes people get paid now. I never played for the money. Never. I played for the game, for the club, for myelf, my family, the supporters. Money? Bottom of the list.

If you just do it for that, you won't be successful. It's impossible.

The stadium was being redeveloped at one end, but it was beautiful, very modern, and you know the thing that really got me? The smell.

I can't explain it, but the smell from the dressing room the pitch, the training pitches, the kit - everything just smelled of . . . football.

It was like there were no distractions. Everything was just set up to play these games and win these games.

The grass was cut so short, the sun was shining and immediately I got the English atmosphere that I'd seen on television.

OK, this was summer and the sun didn't last for long, but . . !

In Holland and Italy, we trained hard - very, very hard.

In England, we had so many games that the training intensity was less. There was less time to recover and work on things, you figured it out in real matches, which was tough but again it helped you in the end.

You had to see situations in real games - not on the training pitch.

You'd have the lights, the noise, the opposition - real situations. Not on a clipboard.

So that was harder, but better. You learned fast because you had to - and I loved that.

Like being back on the street in Amsterdam, you just want to play.

The one thing I found was that most teams in England back then played 4-4-2, so it was less tactical than in Italy and Holland, but Frank could mix it up and play five in midfield and three at the back at times, so Forest were not a typical team in that sense.

Sometimes Stan and I would talk about things, about where to exploit the space, but really, we had two guys up front and it was a case of 'get on with it'.

I wore number 22 because I'd had number 11 in Ajax and Foggia but at Forest Steve Stone had that number - so I was like, OK, double it - I'll have 22. I wasn't going to argue about it with Stoney!

As for pressure, I didn't really feel it to be honest because I thought I played well in my first game at Ipswich and I scored the winner too, so as a striker, getting that first goal is very important.

It was a decent strike too and I remember seeing the Forest fans going crazy - and there were so many of them.

In Holland, Ajax always had a good support, but the country is small. In Italy, the fans don't travel as much - but when I saw the Forest fans that day, I thought: 'Wow! So many people travelled a long way to see us.'

The sun was shining, stadium was full, they were chanting my name and I felt at home straight away.

You get that support and it gives you energy, it really does. When the sun isn't shining maybe and it's cold and wet and you're maybe losing, you hear that support from the Forest fans and it always gives you extra energy.

It's important to players and if you ask anyone they'll say the same. Positive energy comes from them and the team feels it.

So that day, in my very first game, most of all, I was happy to make them happy.

I played alongside Jason Lee and he was super for me; I wasn't a really physical player, but Jason could win nearly every header he went up for, so it was a case of looking where it would come when he won it. He took the hits for me - thanks mate.

That's how the goal came if I remember; Jason won it and as soon as I got the ball, two defenders were on me straight away - that was what it was like. So fast - zip! - they were there.

But I managed to get it out of my feet, make a little space and side foot it into the top corner.

I really like that goal because it seemed to fly off my foot but with good technique too.

The beauty of that team was that mixture of players who could battle, people who could trick defenders but EVERYONE could play.

Ian Woan was just superb, soooo much skill. What do they say, a left foot like a wand? That's what it was. He was almost like one of those Dutch players that always had soooo much time on the ball, like the defenders weren't there.

Trust me, they were there!

But Ian could make it look like he had all the time in the world; head up, pick a pass, put a cross in - just a top quality player.

Stevie Stone had everything; he could power through the middle, win headers, win tackles, score goals and was never tired. Same with Scotty Gemmill - he would run solidly for 90 minutes and look as fresh at the end as he did at the start - never tired.

Lars Bohinen was in there and again, he had so much skill, I'm sure he was part Dutch.

He was small but tough and if people thought they could get at him physically intimidate him, he would show that they could not do that. He was a strong boy, much more than people give him credit for, but most of all he could play. And again - what an engine. All day, up front, back defending, then up front again. Never tired.

OK, maybe these guys were tired - but they never showed it. If I was a defender, I'd have been thinking: 'C'mon man, take a break!'

But no, we kept going and it was a great team to play in.

I mention these names and I have a big smile on my face. I hope if you're reading this and you remember these guys, you do too!

We played Manchester United next at the City Ground and for me this was what I'd come to England for; packed stadium, playing a big team, great atmosphere - I was just so happy and proud to be a Forest player.

We'd only just come up into the Premier League and they were Champions so people didn't really expect much from us outside Nottingham - but we gave them a good game.

They had Mark Hughes, Ryan Giggs, big, big players, but we were not afraid. We drew 1-1 and in Stan Collymore, we probably had the best player on the pitch that day. Roy Keane came on for United and I remember him getting all sorts of shouts from the Forest fans.

Stuart Pearce had a couple of decent free-kicks and I think that game gave us confidence that we could do OK at this level. They were the

Champions and afterwards we were disappointed not to win - so that shows you what we were thinking. No fear.

Stan was a dream to play with. What can I tell you that you don't already know? If you saw him, you know. Fast, strong, good with both feet, tricky, hell of a shot - HELL OF A SHOT - and a great guy off the pitch too.

I still keep in touch with him today; he's been over to Amsterdam and we've met up several times.

I know he has had issues in life, but who hasn't? And the press always focuses more on someone who is outstanding. And that's what he was - outstanding.

When I was playing up there with him, it was just such a good partnership; we complemented each other - big guy, small guy. But it was more than that. We had an understanding that you couldn't get from training - it was deeper than that and more natural.

I just wish we could have played together longer because he was my dream partner at Forest.

The team carried on playing well and people were waiting for us to get beat.

But no, we would win or draw every week at the start of that season - getting some great results.

Towards the end of September, we went down to Tottenham and won 4-1 when I got two goals.

One was a near post flick and the other I remember because it was a header - they were always memorable for me.

But that one, the cross was low and I had to dive in among the boots to get to it. I thought: 'Ohhhh Bryan . . !'

I only got a scratch. Well, a big scratch!

But, hey, when the ball hits the net and you hear the fans cheer, it's all worth it.

You don't think 'uh,oh! This is going to hurt' you just do it.

If you stop to think, the moment has passed and it's too late. You've missed the chance of a goal - and that hurts more!

Take the hit - give me the goal! That's what I would always think.

The only sad thing about that game was that I had a chance before I scored where I ran and ran from our own half to the edge of the Tottenham area and I thought: 'OK, no challenge so far, I'll shoot'. I got a good connection - but the keeper saved it, a GREAT save.

Otherwise, I'd have had a hat-trick, but hey, I'll settle for the two, especially as we won. That's what counts.

One thing that struck me around that time was going to play Wolves in the League Cup.

This was a team not in the Premier League, but we went there and I couldn't believe it - beautiful pitch, big stadium, full with fans, great noise - for a cup game on a midweek. It was a lot of fun.

You just wouldn't get that anywhere else and again it was something that made me think England is different to anywhere else when it comes to football. People are obsessed.

We won that game and I scored another couple, so it was a great start for me and I was really enjoying everything about the move.

Up to that point in my career, I'd never had problems with injury but around midway through that first season I started to get niggly hamstring problems - and it annoyed me a lot.

I was a bit unlucky with it and maybe - maybe - it was the intensity of the games and the number of games in England. Also, the pitches in England back then were heavier - a lot of sand, whereas in Europe it's more clay.

But overall, very happy times. I remember getting on with Stuart Pearce very well - he was a REAL captain.

He was always checking with me to see I was OK, he had me round to his house and he looked after me.

Don't get me wrong, sometimes he yelled at you if things weren't going well and you thought 'Wow!'

But it always had a purpose and it was OK with me. He's the captain, he has something to say and you listened. Not only did you listen, but you acted on it. Otherwise he would pick you up again - and you didn't want that.

On the pitch we had a bit of a wobble around November when we went a month without winning and again that really annoys me, because if it wasn't for that, we would have finished even higher that season.

We were only 12 points behind Blackburn, who won it and we had a better goal difference. One of the games we lost in that spell was to them so you know, we were close, really close - and what a story that would have been.

Out of the Championship and winning the Premier League? It would have been sensational.

Ian Woan celebrates scoring against Derby with Neil Webb and Robert Rosario

Eye on the ball - Gary Charles in action for Forest

Bryan Roy at Ipswich (above) and spending time on the bench (below)

Nigel Jemson on the ball (above) while Steve Chettle keeps an eye on the action (right)

'I never wanted to leave' - Mark Crossley

Jason Lee makes a stylish point with Steve Stone (above). A more up-to-date look, at the City Ground with the author (right)

Chris Bart-Williams and Steve Chettle get ready to break out the dance moves

The Bartman in Florida

Ian Woan in action

As it was, we picked up and beat Manchester United at Old Trafford. I think we were the only team to beat them there that season, but we deserved it. You go there with no fear, you play your game and you get your reward.

That's always been my outlook. Play good football, without fear and let the best team win.

I was loving playing with Stan, we had a settled team and were going well, but we had another bad month in February, where we didn't win. Again three draws - if we could only have turned them into wins.

But then, we got into our stride again. Leicester away - won. Southampton and Leeds at the City ground - 3-0 both games, me and Stan scoring.

Sheffield Wednesday! At Hillsborough - huge stadium, big crowd, big team. And the result? 7-1 to Forest. SEVEN. Pearcey, Stoney, me two goals, Stan two goals, Lars, outside of boot. Just an incredible performance.

Everything clicked for the whole team in that spell and we played some magical football.

There was so much talent in the team, it made me step my game up. I thought the guys were terrific and that game, the way we found space was the key.

Wednesday had a good side - they weren't relegation level or anything - but when we got in our groove like that, we could have taken anyone on.

Without a doubt, one of the happiest games I ever played in.

Pearcey scored a free-kick that nearly broke the net, Ian Woan scored from outside the box and my first was a great team goal - pass, pass, pass - in on the keeper, goal.

Same again, second goal; Steve Stone has about three guys on him, but still makes the pass to me and I score. That was the team - it didn't matter who scored. No-one was greedy. It was just about the team.

And to see the Forest fans - again many thousands - there, all smiling and signing. It was the best feeling. The type football gives you only on special days - and that was one of them. I'll never forget it.

In our last ten games that season, we won EIGHT and drew two. So like I said, y'know, we were not far away. If only the season had gone a month longer!

So that was my first season with Forest and I couldn't have been happier really - unless we'd won something.

But to come up and finish third? No team has ever done that since. We NEVER felt like we didn't belong. The attitude and outlook of everyone was 'no fear'. It works. Trust me.

I never expected Forest to be so high up this tough league in that first season, but also I never really thought we'd be in relegation trouble.

I knew we were a good team and everything came together for us. So great, great memories for me - one of my happiest times in all my career, that first season.

One thing that people have asked me about is my goal celebration - or sometimes the lack of it.

Stan did the cowboy pistol thing, Pearcey always looked angry (I never understood why!) and Lars could do somersaults.

Me? I'm a laid back guy, a bit Dutch so I never really had anything planned.

It was more on my face what I felt - just a really big smile. I was always so happy to score and if it looked like I was being cool, well, hey, cool is good, so I'll take that!

I think maybe that came from growing up at Ajax, where you're expected to win every single game from 12-years-old. We were taught that when you score a goal, you've just done what's expected of you. Get the ball out of the net and go again. It's a good mentality to have.

Obviously, the big issue we had that summer was losing Stan to Liverpool for a big fee.

When you're playing, the fee is irrelevant - it means nothing. It doesn't change the fact that you've lost all those goals, a great player and a good guy.

The club tried to react by bringing in Kevin Campbell - a tough, experienced English guy - and Andrea Silenzi, an Italian who had not so much experience of England.

A lot has been said about Andrea but we became best friends and I tried to help him settle in. He didn't speak English very well, but I'd picked up a bit of Italian so we spoke quite a bit.

I think it was clear he was not really happy in Nottingham and when it's like that, it's difficult to perform at your best.

Again, a lot of people have said this, but I'm telling you, he was a good player. You don't get to the Italian national squad without being very, very good. He just couldn't show it in England. Whether that was the pitches, the intensity, I don't know.

He never really adapted to the culture and that happens sometimes. But he was also a pioneer - the first Italian in England and I think these days, he would do better.

It's less physical and clubs are more used to helping foreign players settle in. Maybe right player, right club, but wrong time.

Things started well the next season, we won 4-3 down at Southampton and it was everything I liked about England again; full stadium, sunny day, I scored two goals and we won.

I remember Matt Le Tissier got a hat-trick for them - and we still beat them.

In my time in England, he was always one of the best players and I really admired him. Unbelievable talent and if England had Johan Cruyff as coach, he would have had 100 caps and been famous all over the world.

Instead, he didn't get the games that he might have got elsewhere, which was sad. Great player.

The biggest adventure we had in that second season though was the UEFA Cup.

I'd won it with Ajax in 1992 so knew it would be happy time for Forest and I enjoyed every minute of it.

When we started out in Malmo though, the pitch there was terrible; really heavy and bobbly. It was also freezing cold, so not a very good game to watch, but we got the away goal and knew that a 1-0 win at the City Ground would see us through.

Now THAT was a great evening. So, so memorable. The noise, the atmosphere was up there with anything in my career. Really special.

It was sensational and I remember the goal I scored because it was similar to my debut goal at Ajax.

It wasn't just a case of hitting it and hoping for a goal. It was waiting for just the right moment in a split second and aiming it. Yes, some of it is instinct, because it's happening so fast it has to be, but at the same time, you have to take that little moment - tiny fraction - to compose yourself, otherwise it goes over the stand!

Of course, I was lucky that when I did hit it, it was a good connection and it went exactly where I wanted it and then . . . *oh wow!*

The noise, the surge, everything good that football brings.

Just amazing and if you were there, I hope you remember it too. If not, hey, look it up and watch and pretend you were there - it will put a smile on your face, for sure.

When I went off right at the end, it was a great feeling and I felt so much respect from the coach and the Forest crowd; I just felt at home at the club, a great feeling and a deep, deep feeling too.

Amazing fans, amazing night. It still gives me goosebumps thinking about it 25 years later.

Paul McGregor got us past Lyon by being so, so sharp in the box after Stuart had his penalty save and we also got past Auxerre, who were a REALLY tough outfit at that time; Laurent Blanc at the back, so many good players.

They say that about the UEFA Cup that sometimes it's tougher than others, because the players are just coming through and you maybe don't know so much about them.

Maybe they said that about us too though, y'know? Suddenly teams in France and Germany were finding out about Ian Woan, Scot Gemmill, good, good players.

In Germany, maybe they hadn't heard of Steve Chettle, but they knew his name when he scored against Bayern Munich and I thought we did well out there.

In the end, there were too strong for us over two matches, a world-class side.

But again, we had no fear taking on these giants of the game.

Obviously, we were disappointed - really disappointed - with the second leg score but we did well. We'd reached the quarter finals in a year when English teams were not doing so well and we could hold our heads high.

People knew about Nottingham Forest again and they had respect for us. When we got knocked out, I was thinking 'OK, we'll do better next year'.

We need to focus on getting in the European placings in the league and we will be better for it, because for a lot of the boys, it was their first taste.

Frank had shown he was a manager who could adapt and take on these European teams and I thought we'd be back soon.

As it was, we finished ninth and I didn't really have the impact again that I wanted that year.

I'd got injured right at the end of the previous season so had to work all summer and then eventually have a cartilage operation, so things were a bit in and out for me. I think I only played something like 25 games, which was so unusual for me.

We had a decent season, but I thought overall, we were disappointed that we didn't do more.

We had set high standards and I don't know whether it was Stan going, the injury I had, but we didn't do as well.

What I do know is I was determined to do better in the third season; I was strong again and looking forward to it.

But well . . . hey, it was a disaster wasn't it? I couldn't believe it.

No-one saw it coming. We had virtually the same team but then I was injured at the start, maybe making the bench, getting appearances here and there but not getting into a rhythm so it was hard, very hard.

But the biggest mistake that season? Frank Clark left.

I don't know what happened but *that was a disaster*.

That was the breaking point. I found out that Frank disagreed with the board about signing players, but losing him was a mistake.

We had a togetherness and I think he could have got us back up the table that year, I really do.

To then put Stuart in charge as a player AND a manager as well . . . it was just too much to ask.

Look, he was a great player, but come on, let him concentrate on playing. Not everything else. Especially when the team is in danger. It just made no sense to me and that's not criticising Stuart, who did as well as he could at the time, with no experience as a coach.

Spontaneously, he had to change his character and that's hard because Stuart is Stuart you know?

We'd all played with him and loved the guy, but now he had too much to do.

He was always relaxed but then he wasn't and things changed. And he was one of our best players who we really needed too and this was affecting his game because he had to be thinking bigger all the time. I think he's said this himself in the past. But he loves the club, so he would do all he could to help, of course.

It was just the wrong move to lose Frank. It came as a surprise to the squad and for me and a lot of the guys, it was very disappointing, even though we were down the table. We could have come back and I think we would have done.

Dave Bassett came in, but for me, again that was another disaster. The team became very insecure. I don't think I was his type of player and we lost direction as the season went on.

That spirit went a little and for me, I didn't have a good spell at all. Every time I played, it felt like I picked up small injuries so it wasn't the best season for me by a long stretch.

The club brought in Pierre Van Hooijdonk and I played some good games with him, but I think there were deeper problems by then. Confidence was low, you're losing a lot and we couldn't seem to climb out of the relegation places all season. It was really hard and I felt sorry for the fans.

You know, it would have been the second time in not many years they had been relegated and none of it was nice.

Everyone was trying hard but it just wouldn't come.

I was playing some games, not others, and the team was changing a lot to try to find a way out of the situation. It was a pity I couldn't have played more games with Pierre because I think we could have been a good partnership.

I started the game against Leeds late on and came on and scored in the game we were finally relegated.

Pierre got a flick on and I scored a header to make it 1-1 against Wimbledon, but it wasn't enough.

That was my last game in a Forest shirt and I am so sad it was such a bad occasion. The only thing I can say is that I left with a goal in my last game, so hopefully it eased the pain of that day because we didn't get beat.

I didn't realise that would be my last game, but I realised I needed a change and maybe the club needed a change too.

They hadn't seen the best of me in that last year and I wasn't too happy with Dave Bassett as a coach, because he had a different style of tactic to the games that I'd played before.

It wasn't suited to me so I think he was happy for me to go and I was genuinely pleased when Forest came back and got promoted the following year as champions. That was brilliant.

Dave Bassett had a clear view of how he wanted to play and I'm pleased it worked for the club. It would have been great to have been part of it, but it wasn't to be.

I went to Hertha Berlin and the club got a fee for me, so I think it was still a good investment over the three years and I'm proud to have been a Forest player - *very* proud.

The club still means a hell of a lot to me and I loved it there, especially in that first season, with Stan and Frank and Woany and Scotty and Stuart - so many great guys, great games.

The second season in Europe was amazing and I'm just sad that the third didn't hit the same highs because of injuries and the things we've talked about.

But it doesn't dull my feelings for Forest; for the stadium, the history, the club, the city, the energy and the fans.

They took me to their heart and I put them in mine too.

I still look for their results and I've been over to watch games and every time I do, it feels like coming home. It's unbelievable and I just hope they can get back in the Premier League where they belong. They've been away too long because they are a Premier League team - that's where they should be.

In Berlin, I found the training very intense and suffered again with injuries, before coming home to NEC Breda and eventually retiring in 2002.

From there, I went straight to working in the Ajax Youth Academy where I stayed for 13 years.

So really, I just carried on in football for a very long time - I didn't have the break that maybe would have served me better.

Stopping playing is hard for everyone - no matter who you are; even if you just play in the park. That day you stop is hard. For a professional, it's worse.

I've said it before, but there's this addiction to attention that you get.

There are always some people saying *'hey - it's Bryan Roy'*. Then suddenly, you think 'hey, I'm not Bryan Roy the footballer any more - I'm just Bryan'.

When you come to terms with that, it's a good feeling. Very liberating. Freedom. But it can take years.

Then you can start to enjoy your life as this new person in society.

It's not easy and it has unique challenges that people don't always see from the outside.

I try to pass on what I've learned to players these days; sometimes young, sometimes older guys, just to let them know that they may feel like this in years to come, but they'll get through it.

And if they need any help, give me a shout. Hey, it's only me.

*Just call me Bryan.*

CHAPTER 7

# NIGEL JEMSON: FINALLY

Coming on as a sub for a struggling team in the old Fourth Division, facing re-election in front of 1,800 away at Aldershot may not sound too glamorous.

Especially as we got beat 4-0. But for me, it was a massive thing - that was my debut for Preston North End.

I was just 16 years old.

Although I was a local lad, I wasn't actually a PNE fan; Liverpool was my club growing up, but I'd played in a league game at a young age, so I was up and running with my career - and very proud to have played at such a young age.

It's fair to say things were different when I was coming through. There were no academies like there are now and it was a case of playing locally and hoping for a trial.

Luckily, I'd been at a team called Bamber Bridge FC who were very successful at their level and there was quite a bit of interest in a few of us lads there.

Blackburn and Preston were looking and I ended up signing Associate Schoolboy forms for North End at the age of 14, learning under the likes of Brian Kidd and Tommy Booth, who were both in the manager's seat for a while.

It was a tough time for the club and among the five YTS lads they had, I was the only one offered a professional contract, joining a squad that included future Ireland star Alan Kelly Jr and a certain Gary Brazil up front.

That summer after my debut, the new manager John McGrath signed almost an entire new squad, including Sam Allardyce and Frank Worthington. Getting to see Frank's skills up close was a treat every day in training. Anyone from that era will remember him, people used to get to the ground early just to see him do his tricks and keepy-uppys in the warm-up. Unbelievable skill.

I made my full debut at 17 away at Swansea and scored as John revitalised the entire club and led the team from re-election to automatic promotion in less than 12 months.

To say he was a 'bit of a character' is an understatement. He nicknamed me the *'Great White Shark'* (don't ask me why!) before a big FA Cup tie against Newcastle and got me to pose with a rifle, ready to shoot down the Magpies. I'm not sure the press offices would let that happen these days (!) And anyway, when did you last see a shark carrying a rifle??

We did OK up there though and even though we lost 2-0, a certain good-looking, skilful forward caught their eye.

*Yep - they signed Gary Brazil.*

I won Preston's Young Player of the Year award however and soon there was interest in me from clubs higher up the ladder.

Norwich City were the first to put a bid in, which was turned down, and there were a few others in for me including Forest - and Manchester United.

I wasn't keen on a move to United even though a fee was agreed for £250,000 and the deal was set to be done after a two-day trial.

In all honesty, I had to be convinced to go there by John McGrath even at that point.

Don't get me wrong, it's a massive club but, at the time, they weren't renowned for giving youngsters a chance. They were more likely to buy their way out of trouble. *(And did I mention I was a boyhood Liverpool fan?)*

Anyway, I went on the first day, had a chat with Alex Ferguson and played in a practice match with the first team squad - people like Bryan Robson, Norman Whiteside, etc. Big names, great players.

It went OK, but I still wasn't overly sold on the idea when I came home that night.

So I was talking it over with my mum and dad, just about to have my tea, when the phone rang and it was the unmistakeable voice of Brian Clough on the other end of the line: *'Good evening young man, I believe you want to come to Nottingham and play football for me?'*

'Er, yes Mr Clough.'

*'Great. See you tomorrow at the City Ground, 9am. Don't be late.'*

So that was that. I didn't even go back to United for the second day. (I'm sure Alex Ferguson got over it fairly quickly . . !)

The thing is, who wouldn't want to play for Brian Clough? Not only was he one of the greatest managers in the game, but he played brilliant football and had a reputation for giving young players a chance.

So the next day, me, John McGrath and my parents drove down - and yes, we got there on time.

It turned out to be a typical Cloughie meeting.

First off, he got someone to take my mum and dad shopping in the lace market in town, while I got sent off to walk his dog alongside the Trent.

To be honest, I didn't even know what the Trent was at that point!

But I took Del for a walk (or rather he took me) while John and Brian Clough discussed what my contract was going to be for the next four years.

When I got back, I was told to 'sign there' and that was that - I couldn't wait, to be honest.

No hesitation at all - I wanted to play for one of the greatest managers of all time at this massive First Division club so I was like: 'Great, where's the pen?'

It wasn't about the money, that didn't come into it.

No-one remembers anyone for how much money they've got in the bank - they remember you for what you do and what you achieve in your career. That's what drove me on.

I just couldn't wait to get it done and at the end, I sat back and thought: 'Wow, I'm a Nottingham Forest player.' I remember it was all just so exciting.

That wasn't the end of the signing-on shenanigans though as it turned out that Cloughie's greengrocer had apparently recommended me to him after seeing me play for Preston against Mansfield (!).

It was enough for the papers to track down the fella and get me to have my picture taken with him a bowl of fruit and whatnot.

*It beats holding a rifle to a cardboard magpie I suppose!*

I didn't expect to walk into the first team straight away and, probably because I'd had a taste of first team football, I was a bit impatient, so I had a couple of loan spells out at Bolton, then back again to Preston.

I think when you go to a great club like Forest, it takes time to get used to things - not just a new style of play, but also living away from home when you're an 18-year-old lad, too.

It took some adjusting to and that's why I always say people should give any new signings time to settle before expecting to see them at their best.

It wasn't until midway through the following 1989/90 season that I got my chance, after Lee Chapman left.

I made my debut away at Luton on Boxing Day and I must have done OK because I stayed in after that.

We played away at Spurs and won 3-2 and for me as a young lad to be playing these top grounds in front of big crowds was the type of thing you dream about; the noise, the lights, the buzz of it all.

We played Liverpool at home on New Year's Day at the City Ground live on TV; packed to the rafters and fantastic to be on the same pitch as people like Ian Rush, John Barnes and Peter Beardsley.

Alan Hansen was at the back for them with Bruce Grobbelaar in goal - people who I'd watched for years as a kid and now I was up against them.

Once the game starts though, you don't think about reputations or who they are, you just care about getting past them and getting a result.

In the end David Burrows brought me down for the clearest penalty you'll ever see, Nigel Clough scored and it ended 2-2.

I was doing OK and a week later we played Manchester United in that famous FA Cup game at the City Ground where it was said to be the end for Alex Ferguson if they'd got beat.

It sums up my feelings towards United that I came out beforehand and said something like: 'I'd love to score the goal that gets Fergie the sack.'

Obviously everyone remembers Mark Robins scored for them, but towards the end Nigel got a flick on a free-kick, Jim Leighton pushed it straight up in the air and I got up above Steve Bruce to nod it it from about six yards out.

*Get in!* A late equaliser - I'm off celebrating my first Forest goal.

The fans were going mad but next thing, the linesman has his flag up, the United players are all round the ref and he's disallowed it. To this day I have no idea why it wasn't given.

I've watch the replay so many times and thought: 'Really? *Why?*'

(Have a look yourselves if you've got time; it's still on YouTube now. Why *was* it disallowed? Answers on a postcard, etc.)

Who knows what would have happened if that had been allowed to stand? A draw might not have been enough to save Fergie's job and that whole era of United dominance could have been very different.

As a boyhood Liverpool fan, I'm not bitter or anything (!) . . . but come on referee!

After that I carried on a few games up front and we did OK, as I got a decent run and not long after that I got my first goal for Forest.

It turned out to be one of my favourites - and not just because it was against Derby (although that always helps).

I remember going down the line, nipping the ball away from Mark Wright, pelting after it and then hitting it with the outside of my foot past Peter Shilton into the bottom corner.

I remember it like it was yesterday in all honesty, because let's face it, scoring past Shilts is not something you're likely to forget.

It was a great way to get my first goal, especially against our arch-rivals and most importantly - it sealed a 2-0 win for us. Everyone in the dressing room knows about the rivalry between the two clubs and we all know what it means to the Forest fans to win that game so - *is it too early for a football cliche yet?* - I was over the moon.

People might ask what the big difference in training was like between clubs like Bolton and Preston and Forest and the truth is . . . at Forest it was a bit easier!

It's part of the magic of working for Brian Clough; he had ways of getting the best out of people that would seem like madness to others.

Sometimes, if we played on a Saturday, we wouldn't be in until Wednesday.

Other times, you were in the next morning.

There were days when we'd just walk down to the training ground, chatting as we went. Brian would talk to some of the lads as we strolled and sometimes that was enough: *'Get changed lads, see you tomorrow.'*

You wouldn't find it in training manuals these days, but that was the aura of the man and simplicity was his genius.

There were no great tactical lectures. There were just principles: look after the ball, make sure you're always moving, keep it on the ground, everything to feet, help each other out.

No matter where you were on the pitch, if you did these things right - and the guy next to you did the same - you could get out of trouble and get at teams.

People might think it was off the cuff and I suppose by its very nature, parts of it were.

But there was more to it than that and we were always in good shape too. When we trained, we trained properly.

There was no question over our fitness and when you've got people like Stuart Pearce, Nigel Clough, Neil Webb - you're always in no doubt what the standards are.

Garry Parker was there too and I've always thought he was a very under-rated player beyond Nottingham - although I'm sure Forest fans will know exactly how good he was.

So you look at those people and you learn from them every day.

I was living my dream and not long after that United game we went down to Spurs again for a League Cup replay where I got another of my favourite Forest goals.

Garry Parker put me through against Steve Sedgley who was backing up and backing up, right to the edge of his own penalty area, where I managed to leave him on his backside and stick one right in the top corner in a 3-2 win.

Obviously, the more often you do something, the more used you get to it and I felt I was getting to grips with the pace and the standard by then.

Towards the end of that season, we went to Anfield and I managed to score past Grobbelaar in a 2-2 draw, so that was a special goal for me too.

I look back now and have to remind myself that all this was happening before I was 20 which was unbelievable really.

But at the time, it just seemed normal. That was my job, I knew I was lucky to have it and the only way I'd keep doing it would be to work hard and keep learning from the people around me.

Obviously the big highlight that season as getting to the League Cup final and playing at Wembley in front of 80,000 people.

It was just incredible really, the whole experience was just a magical day. You might know that the designer Paul Smith is a big Forest fan and he did the suits for us to wear on the big day. As you'd expect, they were very nice too.

I've still got mine somewhere and maybe - *maybe!* - I can still squeeze into it.

When I look back at some of my old teammates . . . I don't think I've aged too badly! No names mentioned obviously.

Apart from my big mate David Hirst at Sheffield Wednesday. What a goalscorer he was. But if you see Hirsty these days . . . well, he's gone the full Larry Lloyd. Enough said.

That League Cup Final itself was just the stuff of dreams though; beautiful sunny day, Forest fans as far as the eye could see - and scoring the winning goal was just the icing on the cake.

Again, the stuff of dreams really.

If you watch it, some people might say it was an unusual Forest goal as it came straight from a Steve Sutton goal kick. I got a flick on to Nigel then raced round for the return, which he put right in my path.

I knew the defender Earl Barrett was rapid, so I had a foot race with him but then slowed down just before I hit the first shot, which was probably a bit too near to his body.

Obviously, the keeper somehow saved it (!), but the rebound popped up and I managed to slot it into the net.

After that, it was just sheer celebration and madness for the next 20 seconds - absolutely crazy.

To score at the end where the Forest fans were was just unbelievable. I can't really describe that feeling, but I'll never forget it.

For that to be the winning goal was brilliant in the end, even though we'd have loved to make it more comfortable at the time.

There was no great celebration or anything afterwards - we just got on with things - and the next day, Cloughie had us in doing running. Lots and lots of running.

It was a bit like that back then - you never knew what was next, so expect the unexpected. Sometimes you'd lose and get a couple of days off. Others, you'd win and be straight back at it then next morning.

He had ways of keeping your feet on the ground if he thought you were getting too big for your boots and he even said that I was the only person with a bigger head than him.

I don't think I was *(honest!)*. But having had success from an early age, it did make me confident and you need that when you're playing up front.

You can't go out thinking *'I'm never going to score today'*. It's got to be the exact opposite.

And the bigger the crowd, the better I played. I never got nervous - I just wanted to get out there and do my stuff.

There's a bit of a myth that I didn't get on with the gaffer, but nothing could be further from the truth.

There's a famous story that goes around about him punching me after a reserve game at Derby. If I'd have had my way, it would never have got out.

The story's true, but there was no malice in it and it wasn't really a big thing. We were drawing 1-1 in the game and towards the end I'd wasted a decent bit of possession and even in the moment I thought: *'Oh God, I'm for it now.'*

After the game, Cloughie was obviously fuming, as he always wanted to beat Derby at anything - even if it had been tiddly winks.

In the dressing room, he asked me to stand up and said: 'Son, have you ever been hit before?'

I said: 'No boss.'

And he just whacked me in the stomach.

To be fair, I don't think I was the only Forest player who ever got a dig from the gaffer, so I was probably in good company.

They were different times back then and I'd never hold it against him. He just wanted Forest to win. First team, reserves, kickabout in the street - he wanted to win.

I started the following season in the team and hit a spell of good form straight away - scoring five in the first four games.

Around that time, I got a call-up to the England Under-21s and played alongside Alan Shearer up front with Steve McManaman on the wing and lots of good players all over the pitch.

It was a fantastic honour and to have represented my country is a career highlight for me to this day.

You ask any professional footballer and they'll say the same - and they mean it too.

There's something special about pulling on your national team's shirt and it's one that I keep in pride of place at home.

It was a good season for me in the league until around December time, when I got injured, but I came back to score a hat-trick against Southampton in the fifth round replay against Southampton.

Cloughie was very good about being family-orientated and often if I asked permission to go back to Preston after a Saturday game, he'd say 'no problem, see you Tuesday'.

Around that time, I asked if I could go back up North and he was fine about it. We had a reserve game against Derby at the City Ground on the Wednesday night and he said: 'Just come back for that, play 60 minutes and you'll be fine for Saturday.'

So that's what I did, but during the game I twisted my ankle a bit. I was out for a little while and it was a race against time to get fit for the semi-final at Villa Park.

I played in a reserve game to prove my fitness and was on the bench for the semi, which the lads won 4-0. So it was all going well.

I was in and out of the team a bit towards the end of that season in the league but I was told I'd be playing in the FA Cup Final.

So in the build-up, I expected to be playing and had my mind focused on that - as you would expect.

We went down the day before and trained at Bisham Abbey but even at that point no-one knew what the team was going to be.

On the coach back to the hotel, there was a curtain dividing the front and the back; staff at the front, players at the back.

Pearcey got called forward to get a piece of paper from Cloughie and just came back very matter of factly saying: 'Right lads, this is the team.'

He didn't name the line-up from one to eleven, he just said: 'There's three people going to be really disappointed with this. Hodgey you're sub, because he's playing Roy Keane. Lawsy, you're going to be disappointed, because he's going with Gary Charles and Jemmo . . . you're the odd one out.'

At that time, we had a squad of 14 but there were only two subs allowed, so that was it. The gaffer was going without a striker on the bench, so I wasn't going to have a chance to get on even.

It was the biggest disappointment of my career, without a doubt.

I know someone has to miss out, but it was just very hard to take. Words can't really describe that feeling - I was just heartbroken.

I can remember crying on the coach but when we got back to the hotel, all the media were there and Cloughie grabbed me for a photo. He's there smiling for the cameras and I just couldn't really do it. I tried to put a brave face on, but I was in tears.

I remember breaking the news to my mum and dad and even telling them not to bother coming but, of course, they still turned up.

I remember talking to them just as we got off the coach and Forest supporters were shouting: *'Come on Jemmo - another winner today!'*

I think the supporters were surprised and disappointed by the team we put out that day.

I've spoken to so many down the years and I think that if Steve Hodge, Brian Laws and myself had played, we might well have beaten Spurs.

I always seemed to do well against them and had a good scoring record against them.

I had the experience of playing at Wembley the year before and getting the winner. But we'll never know.

Cloughie was always very loyal to the lads that had got to the final, but I'd scored the hat-trick against Southampton so I was hoping that would count for something.

It was just such a big disappointment, I've not really got over it to this day. I never really got an answer from the gaffer as to what his thinking was.

A few years later he was asked why he'd left me out and he just replied: *'Because I could.'*

That's absolutely right, but I'm not sure it's the whole story.

Of course, nowadays, we'd have been allowed more subs and I'd have at least had the chance to come on. But back then, it was two subs and that's it. Absolutely painful.

Come the game itself, I tried to have the best attitude I could. I sat on the bench and was willing the lads to win, of course.

Stuart scored and we were all up celebrating. My best friend in football, Mark Crossley, saved the penalty from Gary Lineker and I was delighted for him - absolutely chuffed.

But obviously the game then got away from us a bit and they nick it with the deflection off Des in extra time.

They were such narrow margins and I just wish I could have had the chance to get out there and affect the game. Possibly it's the not knowing what might have happened that makes it worse.

Having said that, I'm not sure it could have been worse though; I was left out and Forest lost.

It sparked all sorts of thoughts and doubts in my mind over that summer; was I really wanted? Should I stay?

All these things were going on and at the same time, the club signed Teddy Sheringham.

Part of me was thinking: 'It'll be great to play up front with him.'

And another part was like: 'Oh hang on, they've signed another striker. The writing's on the wall.'

The positive outlook won the battle though and I was thinking: 'Well, there's me, Teddy, Nigel and Lee Glover. We're all slightly different players and it's a long season, etc.'

So I got my head down and worked my guts out over pre-season, determined to show I should be in the team.

In the first game, I started up front with Teddy and Nigel as we beat Everton 2-1 with me scoring the winner. So I was flying, things were going well and we had a decent start - beating Notts County 4-0 at their place, too.

At the start of September, we went to Manchester City where we lost 2-1 and I tweaked my hamstring in the last 10 minutes.

The next day, I went in for a bit of treatment at the City Ground and there was a reserve game on. I bumped into Trevor Francis, who was managing Sheffield Wednesday, and he was asking how I was, etc. Then he said: 'I came to watch you last night Nigel, because in all honesty, I want to buy you for Wednesday.'

He then put a big bid in for me of £800,000 I think and suddenly my future was up in the air. Forest were great with me, they said: 'It's up to you. You don't have to go, it's your decision.'

I didn't know what to do, so I went up to talk to Trevor in Sheffield - and got lost on the way.

*In hindsight, maybe someone was trying to tell me something (!).*

I had deep feelings for Forest and was happy there. But at the same time, I wasn't sure of my future at the club.

Wednesday had a great squad at that time - people like John Sheridan in midfield - and I thought I'd be able to learn from a striker like Trevor. The real carrot for me was playing alongside David Hirst who I firmly believe would have been as good as Alan Shearer if not better, had it not been for injuries.

In the end, it came down to a career move and, as everyone knows, I left to go to Hillsborough. Again, with hindsight, I look back now and I should have stayed.

*

Not long after I got there, I was involved in a serious car crash. My ankle ligaments took a battering and there were cuts and stitches everywhere.

It was a terrible time on a personal level, absolutely horrible.

The club had to act and they brought in Mark Bright who did well, so it wasn't really until the end of that season that I got in the team properly.

Throughout my time at Wednesday, I was in and out of the team even when I was doing well, so it was just frustrating overall.

I'd moved up to Sheffield because Trevor said everyone had to live within 25 miles of the ground and I missed Nottingham.

I'd rented my old house out to Roy Keane and Gary Charles and again when I saw the place . . . I'm not sure that was the best idea I'd ever had.

In the end, I thought I'd take a step back to go forward and joined Notts County. They were struggling at the time and within five days of Mick Walker signing me, he'd been sacked. So things went pear-shaped from there almost as soon as I arrived.

It was a bit of a weird feeling to be playing for the 'other' team in Nottingham and looking back, it was a mistake to go there - same as it was a mistake to leave Forest.

I should have stuck it out and seen what happened in that 1991/92 season, especially as Teddy only stayed for one year.

But hindsight is a wonderful thing.

From Notts County, I had a few loan spells at places like Watford under Glenn Roeder and a good time at Rotherham, where I scored both goals in a 2-1 win at Wembley in the Football League Trophy Auto Windscreens Final.

From there I joined Oxford under Denis Smith and had two great years there, scoring loads of goals before the club hit financial trouble and had to sell me.

I went to Bury for £100,000 under Stan Ternant, who was very direct tactically - so it wasn't quite my style. Then when he left, Neil Warnock came in - and I certainly wasn't his style either (!).

To be fair, Neil was great. He had me in and said: 'Look Jemmo, you're a good player and a lovely fella, but it's not going to happen here.'

From there I had a short spell in Scotland with Ayr then went back to Oxford for a while before Kevin Ratcliffe got in touch to take me to Shrewsbury.

I had three great years there and ended up as top scorer in the FA Cup in 2003 after a famous giant-killing against Everton.

Sadly, things ended badly there as the club got relegated and I was driving two hours there and back every day as I was still living in Nottingham - so it was a bit of a trek!

Ian Woan was there as well and we left at the same time really. I trained with Forest for a while again and it was just brilliant to be back around the club before joining Ballymena right at the end of my career.

People talk about the 'Forest family' and that's exactly what it is.

Forest is my club and I still work there, doing match day hospitality and the like.

Even though I'm from Preston, I treat Nottingham as my home now and it's a very special place for me.

I look out of my window and I can see the stadium and every day I think how lucky I was to have played there and represented the club.

For years after I finished playing, Brian Clough used to send Christmas cards not just to me but my mum and dad too and whenever I met him he was always great with me.

He used to help out at his son's shop and my wife would go in sometimes with the kids and he'd say what lovely children they were.

When she told him who their dad was, he just said: *'Oh, you're the unlucky bugger who married him then!'*

Overall, I've lived my dream and I'm incredibly proud to have pulled on the Forest shirt.

Yes, if things had been different at times, I could have played at the top level for longer, but there was nothing unlucky about my time at Forest.

Just the opposite in fact. I was fortunate to have been signed by the greatest manager of all time at one of the best clubs on the planet.

He gave me the opportunity not just to play, but also to score the goal that won Forest their last major honour.

*Let's hope the next one isn't too far away.*

CHAPTER 8

# DES LYTTLE: STILL MARKING

It's funny how things turn out in football and little things can make a big difference - no pun intended.

I was playing for Swansea before joining Forest and we came up against Orient four times when Frank Clark was the manager there; twice in the league, once in the FA Cup and once in some trophy game or something.

It was like I kept being put in front of Frank Clark by the luck of the draw.

Orient had a tricky winger called Ricky Otto *(you may well remember him - great player, good hair)* and I always seemed to do quite well against him and keep him quiet.

Frank obviously spotted this and remembered me so when he moved to Forest, I was lucky enough to get the call.

I suppose if I'd have had a nightmare in those games, it may well have been a different story!

Obviously Brian Clough had just retired, the club had been relegated and it was a bit of a rebuilding job for Frank.

I think he signed Stan Collymore first, Colin Cooper second and me third, so there were quite a few new lads coming in and it didn't really have the feel of a club that had just gone down and was on a bit of a spiral.

You could sense a determination about the place - a confidence that this was a one-season stop in the lower level.

It helped that Stuart Pearce was sticking around, Stevie Chettle was still there, Steve Stone - players with international and top flight experience. So I looked at the squad and always thought we'd have a chance of going straight back up.

To be honest, signing for Forest was a dream come true for me after the journey I'd had.

*(I say 'journey' but I hope that doesn't make me sound like an X-Factor contestant.)*

I'm a Wolverhampton lad, but wasn't a Wolves fan as a youngster. I used to follow Liverpool and loved watching Graeme Souness snapping people in half (in the days when you could get away with that).

You see some of the tackles from back then on late-night repeats these days and you think: *'Bliiiimey, that's a red card for sure!'*

Then you look at what happens and it's *'just a talking-to from the referee'*.

Anyway, I played for my local schoolboys, made it to the county side and eventually signed for Leicester City as a 16-year-old under David Pleat as a YTS kid, doing all the fetching, carrying and cleaning that stuff young lads do. I didn't mind it to be honest, it was part of the process back then.

On the pitch I did well though and I actually got my pro contract early, in the middle of my second year there, along with people like Scott Oakes, who went on to have a good career.

Funnily enough, I wasn't a full-back in those days; I played all my time there as a centre midfielder - in my mind I was the next Graeme Souness *(just without the 'tache)*.

Forest fans might laugh at this with my goalscoring record, but I was in double figures for goals in both my seasons there. Seriously, look it up, I used to bag regularly as a youngster.

I don't really know what went wrong, but half way through my first season as a pro, David thought I wasn't going to make the grade.

It was a bit of a shock, especially as I'd been given a contract early. Maybe they were waiting for a growth spurt. If so, they're still waiting - and so am I.

It was a big blow, but we came to an arrangement on the contract (we're not talking millions here) and I went into non-league the following season with Worcester City.

People might say it was a brave step, but it seemed like the only step for me really.

I didn't have an agent, there weren't loads of clubs banging down the door for me and the non-league scene in the West Midlands was a lot different to what it is now maybe.

There were a lot of decent clubs around at that level and it seemed a lot nearer to league standard.

At the end of the day, I was a 19-year-old lad who just wanted to play football.

I kept the belief I was good enough to make it as a pro and if I did well, people would notice me and I'd get another chance in the league.

Luckily, that's what happened and Swansea came in for me after only a year at Worcester with a £12,500 bid.

I'd enjoyed my time there and playing those 'proper' games with points at stake, against experienced players who knew lots of tricks of the trade was a good learning experience.

It was also in front of paying crowds too, so that was another good part of the learning process.

It had really stung when David Pleat said I wasn't good enough, but it was an early lesson about how brutal the game can be.

So when I got this second chance at Football League level, I was determined to give it everything I had.

I know they've been up in the Premier League since then and have a lovely new stadium, but they were down in the Fourth Division at that time, playing at the old Vetch Field.

It was the manager there - Frank Burrows - who saw something in me and moved me to full-back at Swansea. But again, that move only came about because on the Wednesday before the season started, the right-back got injured in training.

I was supposed to be playing in midfield, but got switched back there to help out - and the rest is history, as they say.

The position came fairly naturally to me and I didn't miss a minute that season for the Swans, playing 64 games in all. At the end of that season, I was named Player of the Year, which was fantastic for me as a young player.

I thought I'd cracked it and when I came back in for pre-season training there was talk of a new contract.

So when I got called into Frank Burrows' office that's what I thought it was all about. Happy days.

Instead, out of the blue, he sat me down and said: 'Listen Des, Nottingham Forest have come in for you, it's a good offer and we want you to go and talk to them.'

Well, once I realised it wasn't a wind-up, it was a no brainer wasn't it? *Nottingham Forest* wanted to sign *me*?

I think the fee was just under £400,000 which I thought was incredible, but for Swansea, it was a huge profit on what they'd paid just a year earlier.

Unsurprisingly, things were sorted out within a day both with the fee and my contract.

I'll be honest, I didn't do much haggling, I just wanted to sign. And, anyway, have you seen Frank Clark's poker face?

I was more like *'give me the pen, crayon, lipstick - anything'*.

It was almost two years to the day since I'd joined Worcester and now here I was at Nottingham Forest.

At the end of that day, I just took a moment and let that sink in.

The first morning, there I was, sitting in a dressing room with people like Neil Webb, Scot Gemmill and Stuart Pearce, Welsh international Mark Crossley and, of course, the big money signing, Stan.

So, yes, a dream come true, really.

In those days, you got changed next to your number so there was me *- a no-name coming from the Fourth Division* - at number 2, sat between Mark Crossley and Stuart Pearce - internationals who were household names.

Luckily, there was no big initiation ceremony - other than me crapping myself about it all!

As if I needed any more pressure, Brian Laws was still there in my position and he was a Forest legend too, so y'know . . . no pressure.

It was an absolute whirlwind; I was in a nice hotel in Nottingham with fancy penthouse up top where me and some of the lads used to get up.

Sytners were giving me a choice of BMWs outside and I was like: 'Wow! This must be what it's like.'

Within a couple of days of me signing, we were on a plane going out to Rimini in Italy on a pre-season tour - I don't think I'd even done a training session by then.

I'd definitely never been flown out to Italy so, yes, my head was spinning with it all.

To top it all, I moved into West Bridgford and strangely enough I used to see Brian Clough around the place. I'd nearly crash the car and think: *'Oh my God, there's Brian Clough . . . just walking about!'*

I don't know what I expected him to be doing, levitating or something. You wouldn't put it past him, would you?

The first time you saw him, you were just in awe really. (And the second time, and the third.)

I think his son had a paper shop near where I was living and sometimes on Sunday mornings, he'd be doing a stint behind the counter. Imagine that these days, one of the greatest managers of all time, helping out at a shop on the weekend.

I introduced myself, but he said: 'Oh, I know who you are young man.'

Again, I was like: *'Brian Clough knows who I am!'*

We'd have a chat for five or ten minutes and he'd sometimes give me some advice about things.

Obviously, I hadn't been there when he'd been in charge, but it was a privilege to get to know him and just to listen about him talk about football. You knew you were in the presence of a football great - in a paper shop!

I think the best advice he ever gave me was the same as he gave to most players: *'Keep the ball on the ground.'*

It stuck with me throughout my career. Simple but effective.

That's how he wanted his teams to play isn't it? Slick, passing football - and it's fair to say he did that brilliantly.

I think the best thing about that season we went straight back up was that Forest had kept the spine of the team together.

Pearcey was still there, Mark in goal, Chetts, Scotty Gemmill; yes, they'd lost Roy Keane and Nigel Clough but with Stan coming in, they'd added a new dimension up front.

Dave Phillips brought guile into the midfield too and was such an experienced player, he could play all over the pitch and never looked flustered.

It seemed a bit strange for me that Forest weren't in the top division, as growing up, they were always up there. That's why it's so weird now that they've not been back for so long - it just doesn't seem right.

No disrespect to some clubs who have been in the Premier League over the past 20 years or so, but when you see a fixture that involves Nottingham Forest, there's a bit more attraction to it than other teams.

*(Especially one beginning with 'D'.)*

I was in the side right from the start of the season, which was a good confidence booster, but when you look back on that season, it wasn't always as smooth as you might think - certainly at the beginning.

I didn't start particularly well either if I'm honest and coming from the Fourth Division and taking Lawsy's place, I remember getting booed a few times.

That was a real bump back to earth for me - the reality of playing for a big team. Standards have to be met - it's sink or swim time, y'know?

I was staying at the Royal Hotel in Nottingham on my own and I remember getting back there just thinking: *'Can I handle all this?'*

In the end, I just had to believe in myself, work hard and show what I could do. I know fans sometimes think players are immune to criticism, but they're really not. If someone's giving you pelters from your own fans, you hear it, even though you might try to ignore it.

Same with cliches; fans might be like *'oh yeah, footballers always say that'*.

But there's a reason for it - that's what we have to do; get your head down, work hard, get through it and show you're a good player.

That was my first three or four games really, the pressure was on.

Anyone who thinks players don't feel that pressure, or don't know when they're not playing well is wide of the mark. No-one needs to be told if they've had a bad game. Believe me, they know.

I also know there's more money around today, but I'm sure some things haven't changed.

When you're out there, whatever you're earning - and we weren't on mega-money back then - doesn't mean anything. You might have a decent contract, nice car, whatever, but more than anything, you want to play, to make the starting line-up, to be a big part of things, to win things. That's what drives you on.

The only thing I could do was stick at it, show how good I could be and look at it like a test I'd have to pass.

Thankfully, things improved and I managed to cement my place in the side.

Brian was obviously disappointed not to be playing, but there was never any animosity between us, no problem at all.

We had a big derby game against Derby for the first home game and we were getting beat until Ian Woan scored a cracker, so it was a bit hairy at times at the start of that season.

We took a while to gel and I think Forest were a big scalp for teams in that division and we had a spell where it was taking us time to settle.

Looking back, that happens to quite a few teams who drop down from the Prem. Some players have gone and others have to get use to the new level as well as lot of new teammates. It takes time.

I remember we got beat 3-1 at home by Millwall and I think that was the game that spurred us into getting our act together.

Maybe it was the wake-up call we needed.

A few days later, we went to Birmingham in the next game - they were pushing at the top of the league and on a great unbeaten run.

Some unknown Norwegian lad called Lars Bohinen *(!)* came in for his debut, Stan was on fire - and we won 3-0.

Sometimes, it only takes one good result like that and you're up and running. Thankfully, that's what happened.

That was at the start of November and after that, I don't think we lost in the league again until February - an incredible run.

In the meantime I got my first goal for Forest, against Charlton on New Year's Day. I can't remember much about it to be honest, other than I jumped over the advertising boards at the Trent End - and got a telling off from the ref! (I don't think he realised what an achievement that was for me - scoring a goal AND jumping over the advertising board? Happy New Year ref!)

I think once you get on a run where you're not getting beat, that momentum just builds and builds. Losses become draws, draws become wins and you just get in a good place mentally.

You just go out thinking: 'We're not going to get beat here today.'

I loved going to tough places like Millwall and Wimbledon where you could have a right go at each other and no-one whinged about it.

You'd go flying into tackles and back then you'd get away with three or four meaty ones before the ref had a word with you.

The wingers knew it was coming most weeks, so they just got on with it. Fair play. Although sometimes a midfield 'minder' might let you know they were on the case with a big hit just to let you know they were around. Again, you just got on with it. No rolling around.

These days, you might do one decent tackle, win the ball, hard but fair - and if the ref doesn't like the look in your eye when you went in for it, you're off. Crazy, really.

You watch some of the old games on Sky now and they'd end up about eight-a-side in the modern era.

*

Ian Woan had a similar background to me, having come up through non-league and he was having a great season.

Left-footed players always look great I think, but he was special in that he could do everything; work hard, simple passes, killer through balls, score goals, the lot.

Over on my side, Stoney was in front of me and he helped me a lot; I'd try and get past him as often as I could, but his runs were that good he often didn't need me.

Then, next thing, he'd be right back beside me, doubling up and helping out in defence - and amazingly he never looked out of breath. Admittedly, he looked about 50 years old, but still . . . *(Only joking Steve - top man!)*

It must have been a nightmare for people who were supposed to be tracking him in games, because he just never stopped running.

Certainly at the start when I was struggling a bit, he really helped me settle. If you're a full-back, you couldn't wish for a better footballer or a lad in front of you - always encouraging, advising, helping out, looking out for you. Just fantastic.

But we had those characters all over the pitch; no-one needs to be told what Big Norm is like - just hilarious as a bloke. Stevie Chettle was so well respected and so steady as a player, you could always rely on him in a battle.

The gaffer had paid £1.2 million I think for Coops and he was another absolute leader on the pitch along with Pearcey.

As a back five, we slotted together perfectly I think; being a unit that plays together nearly every week builds those on-pitch relationships, so you know when to cover, when to hold back, etc.

I learned so much from them in terms of organising, shape, picking up, tracking runs, all the things I'd been doing, just at a new level.

Off the pitch, it was a case of learning when to talk and when to shut up. Even though I was young, I'd been vocal at Swansea, now it was a case of establishing myself and then gradually speaking up again.

The other thing is - and it's often overlooked how important this is - we had such a strong bond in the dressing room.

A lot of the lads had been at the club for years and they really welcomed me in.

Even Stan, who was a bit of a one-off shall we say, was always a big part of the group, no problem. There was no stand-offishness right from the start and that team spirit is a big thing in a long season.

When your back's against the wall and you can see everyone throwing themselves into challenges and putting their bodies on the line, it's just a great thing to be a part of.

Towards the end I think we only lost one game in the last 16 fixtures, which was a brilliant run. Momentum is a massive thing.

We beat West Brom and Derby, who were pushing around the top of the league and we feared no-one really. *(Especially not Derby!)*

Maybe we should have feared Peterborough a bit - I was definitely bricking it when they went 2-0 up against us early on.

That was the game that would seal it for us if we could win and they were right down at the bottom of the league. They might already have been relegated actually.

People talk about pressure and it was all on us that day.

It was one of those classic end-of-season settings; the weather's changed, the sun is out, Forest fans everywhere in shirts and short-sleeves - and us fluffing our flaming lines.

You just looked at all the supporters who'd gone down there and thought: *'Come on, we can't let these people down. We're better than this.'*

Thankfully, we were.

Stan got us back into it, Pearcey dived through a mass of head-high boots to equalise. Some people would definitely have flinched but I think he actually *enjoyed* doing stuff like that.

*And then, well, it had to be Stan didn't it?*

One of his best goals that season to get the party started; on the run, out wide, bang - opposite top corner. An absolute worldie.

For me, it was the first real taste of success as a pro and it was just unbelievable really.

In the changing room afterwards, it's just people hugging each other, singing, laughing and joking - and then you keep realising you're in the Premier League the next season.

Well, for me I *hoped* I would be anyway - I wasn't taking anything for granted.

We went out for a lively night in Nottingham that night. I wish I could tell you more about it but it's all a bit hazy! If I saw you that night - cheers!

I remember I didn't have to buy a drink at all and the smiles on peoples' faces, the singing, the laughs - just the sheer joy of it all. You've got to make the most of those moments when they come around, as a player and a supporter.

Mind you, it was often like that around the town. The people were always so friendly and they'd come up for a chat when we were out.

There wasn't any great barrier between players and fans like there is maybe these days. I think we were a lot closer together.

You'd even see players from other teams out in Nottingham because it was THE place to go out.

There was the club called Black Orchid that we used to go to quite a bit. I'm not sure it's still there now, but we had some great nights out there - it was the kind of place you could have a good night and still have change from a tenner. No wonder it was so popular. Great times.

Of course, back at the football club, we were working hard all the time on the training pitch.

Frank had brought in a fitness coach and I think I was probably fitter than ever when we went up for that first season in the Premier League.

We did all sorts; a really tough pre-season and physically, we were up for it without a doubt. *(Still no growth spurt though.)*

The other thing was that we were mentally strong. We'd got in the habit of winning games and we'd go out to play anyone with no fear. We just knew that if we were on our game, we could compete.

Palace had beaten us to the title the year before, but when we went up, we carried on where we left off and they ended up near the foot of the table.

I think a bit of that comes down to mental toughness and that outlook that Forest *'belonged'* in the top flight. Like I said, they still do.

We still had Stan, we had Pearcey and lots of people who had been there before, so there was this belief about us.

Stan was on a mission to show how good he was and really there was no-one around better than him at that point.

He should have been a fixture in the England team for years and years. It shouldn't even have been a question. It should just have been: 'Who's playing with him?'

He could come short and pick it up, but he could work the channels too with his pace.

I think we started and finished with great unbeaten runs and really the club did everything right. We kept hold of Stan and added extra quality there with Bryan Roy too.

There wasn't a great influx of players so we still had a settled unit that knew each other and the way the gaffer wanted us to play.

Especially at the start of seasons, that's not the case for every team so we were able to get in and make our mark.

We played Manchester United in our first home game, the fans were magnificent and we drew 1-1 so again, that gave us belief at that level, because they were a very good side.

I know I didn't get many, but I always remember scoring against Villa the day before my 24th birthday.

Being a West Midlands boy, I had a lot of my family and friends there and, come on, who doesn't love a last-minute equaliser?

So yes, I remember celebrating that one properly.

Obviously, it was the first time I'd played at that level, so there's always a question mark in the back of your mind about whether you're able to step up.

But I think the togetherness of us helped and, like I mentioned, bringing Bryan in gave us a lift in so many ways.

He was a Dutch international straight out of the World Cup, coming in from Serie A and had played for Ajax, so his pedigree was unquestionable.

*It kind of put my Worcester and Swansea days in the shade, let's put it that way (!).*

You might be worried about someone like that being a bit 'big time', but he was such a lovely guy. His movement and his ability on the ball were just unbelievable.

Trying to pick him up as a defender must have been virtually impossible - and the partnership he had with Stan that season, well . . . I just wish we'd have been able to keep them together for years and years.

I think towards the end of that season we won five games on the trot, including a 7-1 against Sheffield Wednesday at Hillsborough.

(The lads gave me a bit of stick after that because it was me that gave away the penalty for their one goal. *Sorry Norm.*)

I think the funny thing is that it was still less than three years since I'd been playing for Worcester and now there I was at Hillsborough, Old Trafford, Anfield and all the rest in front of 40,000 people.

That was one of the strangest things for me, going to those places and playing against these people who I'd only ever seen on TV before - now I was a part of it.

Ryan Giggs was a very tough opponent, but I managed to play well against him and I think he'd get frustrated *(just a bit!)*, which is always good for a defender when you see that.

David Ginola was another very tough guy to mark; he almost looked at you like you weren't there - not in a snide way, just that he was always going to do what he wanted. Until you stopped him, hopefully.

One of the hardest guys I came up against was Trevor Sinclair, because he played on the left but he was right-footed, the same as Ginola. Those guys could go either way and if you showed them inside, sometimes that's exactly what they wanted.

At least with Giggs, you could show him down the line and have a foot race with him to close the pitch off a bit before he did some unbelievable skill.

But with the likes of Ginola, you might do that and he's gone on the inside and stuck it in the top corner if you're not careful.

So you had to hang back a bit and wait a split second to see what they were going to do. It was all part of the learning curve and a step up from anything I'd played at before.

I think it was a golden era for the Premier League back then; looking back there were so many good players and great teams - and, make no mistake, we were one of them.

I'm pretty sure defenders didn't like lining up against Stan, Bryan or Woany either.

We finished third, which was unbelievable on the one hand, but thoroughly deserved on the other. You finish where you belong and we were the third best team in the country that year - that's in the record books.

As such, we qualified for the UEFA Cup and that was just an incredible adventure to be part of.

I don't want to harp on about my *'journey'* but I'd gone from non league to fourth division to Championship to Premier League and now Europe - all one season after another.

Each time it was a step up, but those UEFA Cup games were something special.

The whole experience of going over there two or three days before, seeing these places, going to the foreign stadiums, seeing the differences in the crowds, facilities and stuff - it was all just incredible to be a part of.

There's this theory that foreign players are better than us and in some ways, maybe they are. We're about pace and power and fitness, whereas they were so technical and tactical in their thinking.

I remember some of those games barely touching the ball - and yet we dug in and came out on top, either on away goals or grinding out a 1-0. I think what we've seen over the years since is that the best

English teams have welded the two things together; they've kept the power and the physicality, but they've added in technical brilliance too.

What got us through those early rounds was the fact we had a better gameplan; we'd defend deep and not let teams get in behind us.

We'd have Jason Lee up front who could hold it up for us and give us an outlet, but even then we were just looking to hold positions and hit teams on the break.

Jason was perfect for that role though; big, strong, never stopped working - he was another one who'd come up from the lower leagues and was determined to make his mark.

This was the days of 4-4-2 so to play just one striker was virtually unheard of, but it gave us that extra body at the back and we just closed up all the space.

I think you could see it on the faces of some of the Auxerre players in particular when they didn't beat us, it was: *'How the hell have they done that?'*

To be honest, we were thinking the same thing!

The final whistle would go and we'd kind of look at each other and go: *'Phew!'*

They weren't exactly great games to watch, but the record books don't show that. Maybe they should say '*defensive masterclass'* because that's what it was really.

The only downside for me was the Bayern Munich game at the Olympic Stadium.

We'd done all the training beforehand and we were just about to go back to the hotel for a nap when Frank pulled me to one side and told me he was going with David Phillips that night instead of me.

That was probably my biggest disappointment as a Forest player, not playing in that game.

I was rooming with Jason Lee and remember going back upstairs and being absolutely furious, thinking: 'Why has the gaffer done this?'

Of course, who put the ball in for Chetts to grab the away goal for us? Dave Phillips.

So maybe Frank knew what he was doing after all. *(Still hurts to be left out, though!)*

Obviously what happened in the second leg was that the goal they scored changed the dynamic of the tie and meant that our counter-attacking gameplan was out of the window.

Suddenly we had to open up to get back in it and, well . . . it's Bayern Munich.

And not just any old Bayern side, the players they had out that night are some of the all-time greats.

But overall, we held our heads up high and I think they knew they'd been in a proper game.

They went on to win the trophy that year, so there was no disgrace about losing to them. It was just disappointing that it all had to end, because it was such an enjoyable run.

*

That season, I think we finished ninth again in the Premier League and were never in any trouble position-wise.

People ask what went wrong the following year and . . . I just don't know. It was just so strange really and if anyone saw that coming they'd be a rich man down at the bookies.

Stan had been gone for a year by then but up to then we'd coped without him.

I think when we needed to get a permanent replacement, no disrespect to anyone, they just didn't fit with us.

I'm not blaming the lads who came in. On paper they all looked good, but maybe we just went a bit too big. I don't know.

No excuses though. We're the players out there and you win as a team and you lose as a team, so it's not just down to this player or that player.

Nor is it down to one particular game. When you look at that season when we went down again, we were struggling almost all the way through.

Frank left around Christmas and that was a really disappointing time.

There were rumblings that things weren't great behind the scenes in terms of Frank wanting to sign players that he wasn't being allowed to get.

Again, I don't know. When you're a player, you're not immune to hearing things and you've got loyalty to a manager, but there's so much going on at a club that you've just got to get your head down and concentrate on your job, especially when results aren't going well.

You can't be distracted by anything else other than what goes on on the pitch.

That's your priority. If you get that right, everything else will fall into place, but unfortunately we didn't do that as a team that year.

When the gaffer went, it knocked the dressing room back a bit for sure and maybe, *maybe,* one or two people took their eye off the ball.

I don't know, but what I do know is that when Pearcey took over, there was no messing.

On a matchday, he'd normally say a few words before games anyway and obviously, everyone had so much respect for him.

He was a great motivator and someone you always listened to.

It was Stuart who put me back in my old central midfield role against Chelsea that proved to be one of my most enjoyable games for Forest.

I was put in as an extra man to pick up Gianfranco Zola. *(No pressure there, eh?)*

Pearcey even told me not to offer myself up for passes when we had possession - just stick to Zola all the way through.

I don't think I touched the ball many times that game. But I was always no more than three yards away from Zola - even going down the tunnel at the end!

It wasn't easy, I can tell you, but I managed to sit on him all game and most importantly we won 2-0, so it was good to know I could still do it in midfield, if I really had to.

I did a similar thing tracking Steve McManaman around that time and he wasn't happy with it either. He was having a proper Scouse moan during the game and at the end he even offered me his shirt saying: *'You've nearly been flaming inside it all game mate!'*

No, I didn't take it - just shook his hand and gave him a big smile.

It was around that time that - out of the blue - I had the chance to leave Forest, as Frank came in for me and Tommy Wright to link up with him at Manchester City.

Tommy went, but Pearcey called me in to tell me about it and just said: 'Des, we need you. You're in my plans and I want you to stay.'

To be honest, that was that and I never really gave it a second thought.

I didn't go knocking on doors demanding a move or anything - in fact, I was just pleased to hear Stuart say such good things about me.

Even when I eventually did leave a few years later, I didn't want to go. I loved Forest, loved Nottingham and didn't want to play anywhere else - especially when Pearcey was in charge and the team was in a battle to stay up that season.

I'd established myself by then and was playing nearly every week. I wanted to do whatever I could to help get us out of the mire at the wrong end of the table and build from there the following season.

Just get through it, strengthen then go again - that's what your aim is.

Results picked up for a while under Stuart but we just couldn't maintain it.

I got a late equaliser away at Sunderland on the volley that I remember well - not just for the goal but also for that yellow away kit we used to wear - *a thing of beauty, wasn't it?*

But I think overall we needed more goals in us as a team.

Obviously the club brought Pierre in, but probably that was a bit late in the day. If we'd have had him firing on all cylinders all through that season, it would have been a different story.

It was my first taste of relegation and it was every bit as hard as I imagined. You just feel like you've let everyone down; supporters, staff, coaches, everyone.

No matter how you think you've done as an individual, you've been part of a collective that hasn't met the required standard and that hurts, it really does.

I think we drew too many games and we didn't really get slaughtered by anyone. I don't know if that makes it any better - if anything it's more frustrating.

In the end though, you can't say we were unlucky to go down, there's no great sob story. Just like when we finished third, you end up where you deserve and we were rock bottom.

We'd had the highs and now we got the lows.

It's painful to think about it even now, but that's what it was.

You've just got to take your medicine, use that experience properly from that point on, or you can get dragged into a downward spiral.

Thankfully, Dave Bassett had the personality, the experience and the players to get Forest back up the following year.

I think one of the things about Dave when he looked at the squad was that he realised we still had good players there.

Even if he'd been tempted to go direct, he might have looked at it and thought that actually he didn't need to, because we had enough in our locker to get us straight back up without making drastic changes to our style.

Yes, we had a 'get-out' ball to Kev Campbell if required, but it would have been stupid to come in and try to change the entire ethos of

Nottingham Forest, especially as we had a squad that was full of good footballers, as we proved that year.

It's funny because I can't really remember much about that season other than the whole momentum again that we built up and having that feeling of *'we're not getting beat'* again.

Pierre gave us that extra edge, but he was different to any striker we'd had up to that point.

Stan could do everything, he was a whippet with two great feet and incredible movement.

Pierre? How can I put this? The ball *had* to be in to his feet.

Anything a few feet either side and you'd be on the end of arm-waving, effing and jeffing and a death stare that could stop traffic from 40 yards away.

I've never met anyone moan so much - and as for working the channels? Yeah, right. Not today my friend, or any day come to think of it!

But when he did get on it . . . what a player.

Again, with the ball at his feet, he could put one in the top corner from 30 yard before the keeper had even moved. I think he scored even more that season than Stan did when we went up previously.

The other thing with Pierre was that he had Kev Campbell around as well. Now Pierre wasn't small, but Kev was so strong it was unbelievable - just rock solid, with an unbelievable work ethic.

If I was a centre forward I'd want someone like Cambs alongside me. He could batter defenders, run all day and score goals too, either foot and be great in the air.

Without him and his work rate, Pierre wouldn't have got so many goals that season, that's for sure.

He was the perfect foil for Pierre really and it was a pleasure to be in that team, knowing we had such goal threats up front. I think if your team's got guaranteed goals in it, you're always in with a chance.

I missed the run-in to that promotion season but at the end, the scenes were just fantastic.

To be part of any promotion-winning team is special, but to do it twice at Forest and be part of a team that actually wins the league was just a privilege really.

You want to look back at your career and know that you've won things, so to get a Championship winner's medal is special, it really is.

I don't think anyone could have predicted what happened next though and it just goes to show any career can be a rollercoaster - up one minute, down the next. *Literally.*

I still look back and think: 'What the hell went on?'

We'd just won the league, yet we let Kev Campbell go and sold Col Cooper - two of the lads who were part of the spine of our team when we were going up to a higher level.

I know it must have made sense to someone somewhere, maybe the accounts department, but from a football perspective, it was ridiculous and set us back right from the start.

Then you've got the Pierre situation to make matters worse and suddenly we went from being a team with a positive outlook to one that was on the back foot before a ball's been kicked.

It really was bizarre but it was a bit like the season when Frank left - it was stuff behind the scenes at boardroom level.

I don't know what was in Pierre's contract; whether he was told he'd be sold if Kev went or if the club didn't do this and that. There was talk of big bids coming in for him and being turned down.

I don't think there's any one person who knows the actual story of what went on.

The version I heard was that he was told he could leave if Kev went, but then a big bid came in and it was turned down.

OK, it's disappointing for him.

Going on strike though? *No.*

It's not something I'd ever do. It's not right and in my mind, you get on with it and you do your best no matter what else is going on.

I think that's what disappointed people the most. We were all in the same boat and we should have been sticking together.

Obviously Pierre eventually came back and had a meeting with the rest of the lads, but there was still a lot of the lads who weren't happy about it.

It had a knock-on effect though and I think that was the point that the changing room mentality took a bit of a hit.

The atmosphere wasn't great at that point, which was crazy coming off the back of a promotion season - we should have been buzzing.

But of course to sell him and keep his value up, the club had to play him. If he'd been sitting in the reserves, the transfer fee would have dropped, so it was an absolutely bizarre situation.

You've got your star striker scoring a goal against your big rival and most of the team won't celebrate with him.

Don't get me wrong, I got on really well with him as a person and really what went on was between him and the club. I can see it from both sides, and if he didn't want to be there, the club should probably have just got rid, but going on strike? No. It's not on.

Quite a few of the lads, the senior players, were saying he shouldn't be playing, but of course, we needed him. It was all just a mess really and I wish it had never happened - any of it.

Personally, it was an in-and-out season for me, very stop-start all the way through as I was bothered by an ankle injury.

I started against West Ham early on but came off after 30 minutes, tried to get fit again and came off the bench a few times.

I started against Wimbledon at the City Ground, but I was struggling, so I went out on loan to Port Vale, who were at Championship level at that time. To be honest, I just wanted to get some games under my belt and build up match fitness.

Forest were struggling in the Premier League but when I came back it was just bits and pieces again for me - the odd game off the bench, the odd start.

I understand it to a degree; when a team's struggling, the manager's under pressure and looking for something to turn things around and trying all sorts, but whatever we did that year just didn't work.

In the end, Dave went and I made my last appearance for Forest away at Villa Park under Ron Atkinson where we got beat 2-0.

We actually played OK though we didn't get the result - that kind of summed things up for us.

I was on the bench for the last few games but didn't get on, which was disappointing because if I'd known I was going to be leaving, I'd have loved to be on the City Ground pitch at the end to say thank you to the supporters, because they'd always been great with me.

They'd given me time, backed me - and even put up with my body-popping down at the Trent End *(hey - I've still got the moves!)*.

At the end of that season, David Platt took over as manager and it was all-change, really.

People ask what he was like, but to be honest, I only spoke to him about three times. My contract was up over the summer and he called me in for a meeting.

We didn't get as far as his office; we ended up talking on the car park, where he said he wanted me to 'prove myself' to get a new deal.

I thought: *'What's he talking about? I've been here six years. Has he not been watching TV? Does he not know what I can do?'*

He also came out in the press and said something along the lines of having a clean sweep and clearing out the old guard.

It wasn't just me, but also people like Chetts and Ian Woan.

I thought it was daft to lose so much experience and people who cared so much about the club but, well . . . there you go.

So everything was looking bit uncertain at Forest and a few days later, Watford got in touch with me. They'd just been promoted back to the Premier League under Graham Taylor and were keen to have me.

It was a case of either staying at Forest to 'prove myself' to a manager who wanted rid of the old guard - or sign for Watford in the Premier League?

*It sounds like an easy decision, but it wasn't, because of my feelings for the club.*

I didn't want to leave - if I'd had another year on my contract at Forest, I'd have stayed and seen how things went. You never know, I might have proved myself to David Platt after all.

But it was clearly time to go - so I left for Watford. Players often say this, but genuinely money didn't come into it.

If I'd thought I'd get a proper chance under the new manager at the City Ground, it would have been a different story, but with everything David Platt was saying, well . . . I knew I had to go.

Look, managers come in and do these things and if that's what he thought was best for the club, then it's his prerogative.

The sad thing was that it didn't work out well for Forest in the end and he left a couple of years later with them still in the Championship.

Even when I left, I wanted them to do well. I still do now. It's a fantastic club and a big part of my life.

I went on to have a good career with West Brom and Northampton for a while before finishing off in non-league, including two happy years back in Worcester where it all began.

Obviously I still look out for all my old teams' results, but especially Forest.

I know it's hard to think about, but recently when everything came down to that one crazy night in the Championship, I had my three exteams all chasing a place in the Premier League - West Brom, Swansea and Forest. What are the chances?

I couldn't believe it when Forest were the ones to drop out. It was absolutely gut-wrenching, but I'm sure Forest fans don't want to even think about that.

The only positive is that I still think they've got everything in place to be a well-established Premier League club again and I genuinely think they'll be back there soon. I certainly hope so.

These days, I'm a teacher *(stop laughing at the back)* at a good school in Shropshire, where I'm director of football.

A lot of the time, the pupils don't know that I used to be a professional, but occasionally there'll be a picture pop up of me fronting up to Eric Cantona or something and they'll all start firing questions at me: *'What was Cantona like?' 'Do you know Ryan Giggs?' 'Who came up with that yellow away kit?'*

It's funny because the first answer I give when they ask who I played for is always 'Nottingham Forest'.

That's my team in my mind and I'll never forget those days at the City Ground. How could you?

It's a special place, a special club and it was an absolute privilege to have played there.

*You know how it is - you never lose that loving feeling.*

CHAPTER 9

# GARY CHARLES: HAPPY DAYS

You might not have spotted this, but I've always been blessed with young looks. (Well, until recently!)

People used to look at me and ask why I was playing in age groups a couple of years older than me, when I was actually the same age as everyone else.

I've never been a big lad either and even though I spent time with Arsenal and West Ham as a youngster, they let me go because they said I was too small. *As if.*

I'm a boyhood Hammers fan too, so I was gutted.

I'd always been a right-back, so I thought my frame would have been an attribute as I was a good runner, quick and covered the ground well to get forward.

I never did get that growth spurt to turn me into a Stuart Pearce psycho-type, but I made the best of my physique and I think I did OK.

I was about 15 and, having been blown out by a couple of big teams, I was all set to sign up for a YTS at Leyton Orient under Frank Clark. It was London, it was a foot in the door and I was happy with that, to be honest.

But then just before I was due to sign, I was playing for my local team when a Forest scout spotted me and asked me to come up for a trial. Well, it was a no-brainer so I packed my bags, polished my boots, checked the map and headed north.

It was meant to be a two-week thing, but I signed up for a YTS on the first day and really, it was a dream come true.

It wasn't just the first step to being a footballer but also a great adventure. I grew up in the East End of London and, without being too harsh, Nottingham was a lot nicer than where I was from.

There was the river, the greenery, a bit of countryside - and the people were really friendly.

I'm not knocking London, but there's a different type of warmth away from the capital isn't there? People talk to you out of the blue - proper conversations too, *me duck.*

I was in digs just over the bridge from the City Ground and, while it was tough in a way to be away from home, I just remember being excited by it all.

*

I can't recall exactly when I first met Brian Clough, but he just was always around - you were always *aware* of his presence.

One of the first things he said was that he liked the way I ran and I think he could see something in me that he could work with.

He had a few nicknames for me (!) but at one point, he told the press I was like a gazelle. I know they're quick, so I'll take that.

The truth is, I just loved to run. I was always light on my feet and sometimes I'd do twenty box-to-boxes after training on my own just because, well . . . I liked it.

Some of the lads used to look at me like I was mad, but that was my game really - getting up and down for 90 minutes, being in the right place at the right time and seeing if the guy you were up against could keep up.

I'd go on long distance training runs sometimes, mile after mile, just keeping going, building up stamina.

I played up on the wing a few times, but didn't really change position in the team much - I was happy at full-back.

I did sometimes play as a sweeper in the Forest youth team and also centre half for the reserves in the Central League.

It may have been a challenge for me in the air, but it gave me an insight into what the lads in the middle were looking for from the full-backs.

Those reserve games were great learning experiences and I'm sure a lot of people from back then would say the same thing.

I was 16, playing in front of several thousands fans at the City Ground against some established senior pros.

For a young lad to be up against someone like Mark Walters at Villa, with everything he could do, well . . . *you can imagine how tough that was.*

What an opportunity though to see the levels you needed to be at; to get a feel for the pace of the senior game, the tricks and the flicks - all that stuff stood you in good stead.

But in the back of your mind, you'd do 90 minutes against Mark Walters and think about the senior pros: *'Blimey - they can't all be this good can they?'*

I know times have changed and academies are totally different to my era, but if you talk about 'development' those games used to turbo-charge you. You learned because you had to learn. And you had to learn fast.

My YTS wage was £25-a-week but we could virtually double our money by going over to Brian Clough's house, raking the leaves, doing a bit of gardening - anything he wanted really.

If I made any extra cash, I used to send it back to my mum.

Brian's wife Barbara would fetch us sandwiches and he'd sit and talk to you about football, life, the issues of the day.

Despite my youthful looks back then, not long after I arrived at Forest, he asked me if I was married (!).

I rang my mum that night and she said: 'He does know how old you are, doesn't he?'

I said: *'I think so mum, but now you come to mention it . . .'*

I was 15.

I think what he was trying to say was *'get married young, get settled down and it will be good for you'*. That was the way he looked at it.

I was about nine-and-a-half stone most of the time and he was always keen for me to bulk up a bit. At hotels before away games, he used to come round and get me to show him my plate to make sure I'd finished my meals.

If I didn't have any greens with my dinner he'd shout at me like I'd given a goal away.

At one point, he threatened that I'd have to go and live with him if I didn't start to put weight on.

Even now, I've not got a very big appetite but Brian would have us round for breakfast and you'd have everything in there - the Full English and more. Three Shredded Wheats all round.

I'm pretty sure it's not like that in the modern era, but looking back, it's incredible how lucky I was to have those experiences. I'm not being nostalgic when I say I wouldn't have missed it for the world - it was genuinely one of the happiest times of my life.

The gaffer always took an interest in you and how you were doing. People often remember the harder side of him and some of the outlandish things he did at times, but he was also very caring and I think he felt a responsibility for us young lads who were away from home.

He used to get me to walk his dog - *Del* - along the Trent and I used to let it off the lead for a quick runabout.

It's a famous story, but one time, it just went and I lost it completely, it just ran off and I thought: *'Oh my God - I've lost Brian Clough's dog!'*

It felt like I was out there for hours looking for it before finally giving up and heading back to face the music.

I'll be honest, I was bricking it. Who wouldn't be?

But when we got to the City Ground, I could hear this barking and there was Del - he'd run straight back to the ground and was sitting in Cloughie's office.

I played it cool: *'Just bringing the lead back, Mr Clough.'*

Thank you, Del. And thank God you couldn't talk.

*

I also used to earn a few quid cleaning the players' cars and Garry Birtles would always give you a Christmas bonus - he used to say the only time I ever cleaned them properly was when Christmas was coming up. *(No comment!)*

We did other tasks around the ground, mopping up, making the tea, all that stuff and, of course, we cleaned the players' boots. My four were Johnny Metgod, Garry Birtles, Gary Fleming and Gary Mills. So every day I had to put their kit out and make sure their boots were spotless. They were all OK with me, a bit of football banter every now and again but really friendly mainly.

In fact, if you asked me which part of my career I enjoyed the most, it would be those days on a YTS.

It was a brilliant time; learning every day, being part of this great football club with a great family spirit.

No money, no great pressure, no luxuries, living in digs - just Forest, football, family and friends. I didn't need anything else.

All those little tasks gave us an opportunity to go into the first team dressing room and that was a big thing for me. I was fascinated by what they spoke about, what they did behind that door, how they acted. I always wanted to learn from them.

I remember Ian Bowyer used to always throw me out if he caught me listening in there: *'Get that little Cockney out!'*

The funny thing is, the conversations were really just the same as us young lads were having in our dressing room; who should have done this and that, who was marking who - but it always sounded better coming from them.

These players had been there and done it; established themselves as professionals and won things at a big club like Nottingham Forest.

If ever we finished before them and some of the lads would go back to get changed, I would always sit and watch the first team, just trying to pick up things from them, anything that could be useful for me to learn from.

I'd never turn down an opportunity to watch them, rain or shine.

On top of all that, we had one of the very best ex-pros watching over our group.

Archie Gemmill was the youth team manager and he used to lead by example; he'd join in all the running and I don't know what age he was by then - no-one ever dared ask - but he was always up at the front.

You'd think: *'If he's like this now, imagine what he must have been like as a player.'*

Everyone knew what he'd achieved in the game and his advice about things and his football knowledge was incredible.

Again, he was Forest through-and-through and I just tried to hang on every word. That's how it worked; if you switched on and listened you realised you were getting the best football education around, from the best teachers in the country.

Of course, the game was very different back then and there was a drinking culture that was part and parcel of it.

The manager had come through that 1970s era, when it was possibly even bigger, so largely things were just accepted - apart from drinking straight out of bottles. That was a no-no for some reason.

At the time, I didn't realise how alcohol would play such a big part in my future in such a negative way. I could drink or I could go weeks without drinking. I still had that control.

Either way at that time, my career was moving forward - probably faster than I expected.

My chance to play in the first team came early even if it was only for a brief period at that point.

I was just 18 when I was called up for Forest against Coventry in 1988, but before that I had to go through one last trial.

On the Sunday before, I played for Cloughie's son Simon's team, AC Hunters, in the Derbyshire League as a ringer - on the right wing.

We won and I scored a couple of goals but the boss wasn't impressed. *'I could have scored those two,'* he said. I wasn't going to argue otherwise (and anyway, he probably could have, to be fair).

Nevertheless when I got back in on the Tuesday, I was named in the first team for a League Cup game against Coventry at the City Ground.

I don't know which emotion won out that day; the excitement or the nerves. Call it a draw.

On the night, well, you've just got to get on with it. That's what you're there for and although it's a big thing, you've just got to handle it. That's what you've worked for and that's what you're there for.

I think there was an injury crisis because I played right wing and it was just a fantastic experience to be in front of a big crowd in a 'proper' game.

Again it helped that we'd played those Central League games at the stadium so it was fairly familiar surroundings, but obviously with 20,000 on, a lot noisier than I'd been used to.

I got the odd round of applause for doing stuff well and I thought: 'Yeah, I can get used to this!'

When it comes down to it, the whistle goes and it's a football match. I must have done well overall, because I was named man of the match if I recall correctly, but the most important thing was that we won 3-2.

That weekend I kept my place in the team for my league debut - away at Arsenal. If I'd been thinking things were going OK, I had a bit of a reality check there; we lost 4-1 and I was taken off.

So that brought me back down to earth - and the reserves.

I wasn't completely out of the picture though and Brian would often take young lads with the first team to away games, just to get a flavour of what it was like; carry the kitbag, help out if anyone needed anything.

Sometimes he'd have you on the bench next to him and this was at a really young age, don't forget.

So you'd be there, next to one of the greatest managers of all time, getting a ringside view of how he operated.

At times, he'd even ask your opinion on things and no matter what you said, he wouldn't be disparaging. It was quite intimidating, but I just tried to be honest.

Looking back, I think he was trying to see how much you were picking up on games as you watched, whether you could detect patterns of play and things.

It was as brilliant as it was fascinating and sitting there with him, Archie and the coaches was a fantastic football education - no-one could wish for more.

And it wasn't just football. There was a family spirit at Forest that meant the players were part of a bigger team. Everyone knew everyone's names and when it was the tea lady's birthday, for example, Cloughie had us all sing *Happy Birthday*. There was a great togetherness about us.

We were learning about respect, about how to behave and how to value things that are important in life. How to make the best of your talent no matter what it was.

I used to put his kit out for him and run him a bath in the referee's room after training.

He'd always ask me how I thought I'd played at the weekend and you were always nervous about what to say.

One day I was in there and he said: *'Oi . . . young man. Do you think you're good enough to be a pro for Nottingham Forest?'*

'Err . . . yeah.'

*'Well go and tell your mum you're going to be a professional footballer.'*

And that's how I found out I was getting my first contract.

I can honestly say I never even looked at how much I was going to get paid, but I said to him: 'Can I just ask for one thing please?'

He looked at me a bit surprised and barked: 'What do you want?'

I thought: 'Oh my God, I've done it now.'

But having gone that far, I had to say what was on my mind: 'Can I wear a blue tracksuit like everyone else?'

He laughed a bit and said: *'Course you can son. No problem. I can sort that out for you, leave it with me.'*

I got in the next day to find twenty-odd blue tracksuits . . . and one bright red one bang smack in the middle with my name on it.

You can imagine the stick I got from the older lads after that.

*Back when I was starting out Forest always seemed to have players in the England set-up. Stevie Chettle played quite a few games for the Under-21s and was always someone to look up to, having come through as a YTS just before me. I got a call-up in 1989, too.*

*A young Kevin Campbell was bursting onto the scene and Carl Tiler was also around, so there were some future Forest players on the radar. I remember one Under-21 game I played and the front three was Alan Shearer, Steve McManaman - and Nigel Jemson.*

*I think it ended 0-0 but the fact we didn't score definitely wasn't down to Jemmo. (Well, that's what he told me anyway!)*

*There were people like Neil Ruddock, Lee Sharpe and David James around. I think David took over from someone called Mark Crossley, but it couldn't have been our Mark Crossley because, as everyone knows . . . Big Norm is Welsh. Isn't he?!*

*Those games were under Dave Sexton and then Lawrie McMenemy and they were both really knowledgeable football people.*

*I loved those matches and pulling on the England shirt was a massive thing. It's something that no-one can ever take away from you at whatever level.*

*When I got a call-up to the senior squad a couple of years later it was funny because we played New Zealand and there was me and Stuart as full-backs, Des in the middle and Chris Woods, who started out at Forest, in goal. So four out of five had Forest connections with only Mark Wright between us in the middle.*

*Nigel (Clough, not Jemmo) was on the bench that day too and it was great to be part of that England set-up even if it was only for a couple of games. I got an assist for a David Hirst goal in that game and would have loved to win more caps, but for whatever reason, it didn't happen.*

*I found Graham Taylor a really nice man and the players liked and respected him. I think he was unfairly treated by the press and it was only later on that they realised just how good he was. But by that time, of course, he was no longer in 'the impossible job'.*

Later that season, I went out on loan to Leicester under David Pleat, who was a very different character from Brian Clough, but a great manager all the same and it was a good experience. I was playing for them nearly every week and I was still only 18, so to get that chance to play in front of big crowds at the old Filbert Street ground, where the fans were right on top of you, was another learning curve for me.

Gary Mills was there at the time and he used to take me in, as I hadn't passed my driving test, and again it was great just to pick his brains, remind him that I used to clean his boots not that long ago - and chase up my Christmas tip.

It wasn't really until the 1990/91 season that I got a proper run in the Forest first team and even then it was towards the second half of the season.

I filled in for a couple of games for Brian Laws when he was out; Crystal Palace at home *(lost 1-0)*, Luton Town away *(lost 1-0!)* and it wasn't until late March that I got a proper run of games.

Even then it took a while before I was on the winning team in the league - 2-0 at home to Sheffield United. *Thank you, Tommy Gaynor.*

Tactically, we always tried to play the *'Forest way'*; ball on the ground, neat passing and play out from the back.

It wasn't something that was drilled into us in training sessions or tactical meetings, it was largely off-the-cuff and just seemed to be second nature when you got into the first team.

Brian Clough would always tell you: *'Look after the ball, cherish it, don't let the other side have it - because they won't be as nice to it as you will.'*

I think he signed players who could all play; people with good control and that ability to adapt on the pitch to different opponents, tough situations. He watched people and could tell if they had what he was looking for. If so, he would take that and work on it with you to make you better and better.

That, for me, was a big part of his genius - he trusted players. When you're in a game, it's not about the tactics so much as about the people that are out there and how they adapt.

There are times when you might be thinking: 'Hold on a minute, they're on top of us here, what can we do to change it around?'

Yes, the manager can influence that, but largely it's down to the players in the team to sort it out.

Get the ball, find a teammate with a pass, move and do it again. It sounds simple, because as a philosophy . . . it is.

Putting it into practice when there's 11 other guys getting in the way? That's the tricky part.

Normally the toughest thing is finding space, but once the other team lets you have it, then you're in business.

Not long after I got in the team we played Chelsea at home and we were just able to get into our rhythm; pass, move, pass, move.

We ended up beating them 7-0. Not long back I was just falling asleep one night when the game popped up on Facebook and I ended up watching the entire game. What a performance.

It's funny to hear all the analysts these days talking about teams playing out from the back and the *'modern way'*, etc.

*Watch that game - we were doing it back then.*

We had eleven good players who were comfortable on the ball, knew what they were doing and could play through most teams. Just ask that Chelsea side.

A few days later we put five past Norwich, again without conceding a goal. Thirteen goals scored in two games with none conceded - it doesn't get much better than that.

You might think it was easy for a young lad going into the team when they're playing like that but it wasn't. I knew the standards to be maintained and desperately didn't want to let anyone down.

No-one did and that's part of what drove us on.

*

I think one of the days everything came together was the FA Cup semi-final that year against West Ham at Villa Park.

Obviously, it was a huge occasion but especially for me as a boyhood Hammers fan as a load of my friends and family were in the West Ham end.

Whether I was playing for Forest or not, they were blowing bubbles - and spitting feathers after Tony Gale got sent off.

I don't think my brother spoke to me for about six months after that game, playing West Ham was the only time he didn't support me.

But what a day that was. When you start out, the dream is to play first team football, but then to do that and so quickly be in these massive games . . . it was just incredible.

I don't want to sound flash, because I'm really not, so bear with me on this and I'll be as straight down the line as possible.

The day after my 21st birthday, I scored in front of 40,000 at Villa Park, packed with Forest fans, alongside people like Roy Keane and

Stuart Pearce, to help us get to the FA Cup final - with Brian Clough as our manager.

Ask any young lad how they'd feel about that. To say *'it's the stuff dreams are made of'* doesn't really do it justice. It was crazy really.

And yet, it had somehow become the new normal very quickly. It had to be. I was 21 years old - if I stopped and thought about it too much, it might well have blown my mind.

Yes, I'd worked hard but I was also a lucky lad.

I played at Wembley in three finals for Forest at such a young age, when a lot of players can go through their entire careers without playing there once.

It's strange looking back because at the time you don't really take everything in. The Cup Final back then was massive; the whole country used to stop and watch it, with helicopters following the coach on the way to the stadium, wall-to-wall TV coverage - it was incredible.

Prince Charles and Princess Diana were guests of honour, but to be honest, I only remembered that recently when it popped up on TV. At the time, you're so focused on the game, it's a case of: *'Oh, hello. Right, let's get started.'* You just want to get going.

Brian had thrown a bit of a surprise as I'd not played the last few games of the season, but as ever, he didn't actually read the team out.

Normally, someone just stuck it on the wall and you saw if you were in that week or not. If not and if you were feeling brave you might - *might!* - make the dreaded walk down to his office to ask why. Not many did.

For that game, Pearcey was handed the team sheet on the coach after training and went through it with us.

I got the nod over Brian at the back, while Roy Keane was in midfield and Tommy Gaynor up front. Steve Hodge and Lawsy were on the bench and, as there were only two subs in those days, Nigel Jemson was left out completely, which was a bit of a surprise I think as he'd scored the winner in the League Cup final the year before.

The way I looked at it, someone was going to be left out and at the time, I was just excited to be in the team. I think Brian liked to stick with players who had got to finals in cup competitions.

Everyone remembers that year for Paul Gascoigne's injury after making that tackle on me. To be honest, Paul's a mate of mine and it's not really something that I ever talk about. Everyone's seen it. What more is there to say?

He's had his issues since and so have I, so we've built up a friendship and try to look out for each other. Strange how life turns out, isn't it?

It was sad - *really sad* - that he was injured because he was a huge world-class talent, but from a Forest point of view it gave Pearcey the chance to hit that free-kick which was as good as any you'll ever see.

After that, Paul went off for them, Nayim came on and it was a tough, tough game. Very hot, a big old pitch and a proper cup final. I don't think it was a tactical battle - just two good sides going at each other.

Obviously, Norm saved a penalty from Gary Lineker but eventually they equalised and it went to extra time. One or two people might have thought it strange that the manager didn't come over to us to speak, but the coaching staff were there, we knew what was needed between ourselves and we knew the gaffer trusted us to get on with it.

I don't think he would or could have come over and made a massive change or difference to anything at that point.

And look, Terry Venables was giving Spurs all sorts of instructions - that was his style and he was a great manager.

But in the end, it didn't come down to which manager did what. It came down to a misdirected header off Des that flicked over my head and was in the back of the net before I could react.

I've watched it so many times and thought: *'Why didn't I jump?'*

It still gets to me, but of course, when you look at it properly, it's a split second thing - even if I'd have got off the ground, the speed and the angle would have made it virtually impossible to get to.

*Ahhhh* . . . I guess it's the fact that I didn't jump at all.

I don't know. I probably wouldn't have been able to get to it.

Maybe if I'd have handballed it? I don't even know if I'd have reached it even then, y'know?

*But as you can probably tell, it still drives me mad.*

It was just one of those things that happens in football; the beauty of the beautiful game - unless it ends up in your net.

I was gutted for Des, who's like a big brother to me. Thankfully, he's a strong character so he could deal with it and he was such a great player anyway. I know Forest have had some good players since our day but nearly 30 years on, it's still true what they say - you'll never beat Des Walker.

We were disappointed for the manager, because we really wanted to win the FA Cup, not just for ourselves and the club, but also because it was just about the only trophy he hadn't won.

But you've just got to go away, get yourselves sorted and get ready for the next season.

*I make no secret of the fact that I've had my issues with alcohol. In fact, it's just the opposite - I hope that by talking about things and being open, I can encourage other people to get help and support for things they may be having trouble with.*

*I've been sober for 13 years now, but still go to AA meetings and do what I need to do.*

*These days I run a company that helps people from all walks of life, not just footballers, but accountants, barristers, you name it. Addiction is a powerful thing and I try to suggest solutions for each person, rather than have a set view, because no two challenges are the same.*

*I talk to young players about the pitfalls they will face in their careers and also deal with agents, as there are times when people would rather talk to our counsellors than bring things up at their clubs. I understand that and my view is that whatever people are comfortable with is fine.*

*It's not about the why's and the how's - it's about people getting the help they need. You don't have to be a footballer. People have pressures and issues in any job and there's absolutely nothing wrong with using the help that's out there.*

*Support like that wasn't really around in my day, but I wish it had been. I truly do.*

*Knowing that someone is out there who can empathise and support without judging you can be a great help in itself and if some good comes from my own experiences, then it's a purely positive thing.*

When August came around, I started in the team and we were optimistic about the season ahead. Teddy Sheringham had come in and was a fantastic player and people like Roy Keane and Scot Gemmill were really establishing themselves in midfield.

Quite early on we played Notts County, who were up in the old Division One with us at that point and I remember a huge Forest following at Meadow Lane, taking over two sides of the ground *(to be fair, it's not exactly a long away trip is it?).*

Gary Crosby put us one up and then we broke away down the right hand side again. Jemmo played a long ball out and Gary just about kept it in play as I legged it past him on the inside.

He rolled the perfect pass into my path and I was able to slide it under the keeper to put us 2-0 up right in front of the Forest fans.

I think that was my first goal in the league and to get it in a local derby was fantastic. I look at my face on the footage and it's just sheer joy. I love that.

We were playing great *'Forest football'* and to get on the end of a counter attack after running so far was just brilliant.

It makes up for all the times you sprint all the way up there, someone loses it and suddenly you're legging back to your own half at full pelt.

The funny thing was we used to train next door to Notts County and sometimes Brian Clough would just walk us over to their pitches and say to Neil Warnock: *'Right, we'll have a game.'*

Neil would just laugh and go along with it because every manager looked up to our gaffer. After all, it's Brian Clough.

The coaching staff would just let us get on with it and you'd end up having proper full-on matches against your rivals the day before a league game, kicking lumps out of each other while the gaffers had a chat.

*

It was a good season for me but I got injured towards the end and was struggling with my hamstrings quite a bit.

What was weird was that we played the Zenith Data Systems Cup Final at Wembley at the end of March and won 3-2 against Southampton, then a couple of weeks later we were back there again for the League Cup Final against Manchester United. I wasn't even 22 and I'd played three Wembley finals in the past year.

Pearcey was injured for the Manchester United game and Brett Williams was filling in. I'd had trouble with my hamstring, but I honestly thought I would be OK. Of course, not long after Brian McClair scored for them I had to come off - I was absolutely gutted.

Luckily, Brian Laws was on the bench so it was a straight swap but what with the injury flaring up again and us losing 1-0 it was another disappointing day under the twin towers.

Still, we got to keep the ZDS trophy as they packed it in that year, so y'know, out of the three . . *we got the big one.*

I didn't play again for the rest of that season but we finished eighth and there was no sign of what was to come the following year.

*I'm not saying we were complacent, just that no-one saw it coming.*

Roy Keane's still a pal of mine and we talk about it now and then and it bugs the hell out of both of us. We look back and think: *'What the hell happened?'*

You look at the team on paper, you look at the manager and the coaching staff and you just think: 'That's crazy.'

Maybe we fell into the trap of telling ourselves we were too good to go down - until results told us otherwise. You see that happen to teams sometimes, but I just never thought it would happen to us.

I'd popped my shoulder and didn't really play that many games up until about February, by which time we were stuck at the wrong end of the table.

I missed the last five games of the season again and just had to watch from the sidelines as this great club slipped from the top flight and one of the greatest managers of all time was given one of the greatest send-offs from the adoring Forest fans.

What can you say about that day? It was surreal. A team being relegated and the fans never stopped singing the manager's name. I don't think it would happen for anyone else.

And mad as it sounds, it was fully deserved for everything Brian Clough had done for Nottingham Forest.

I don't think you'll ever hear anyone from back then who spent any amount of time with him say a bad word about the gaffer. How could you? He was everything to us. It was all just a sad way for it to end - and, no, *'sad'* doesn't really cover it. Heartbreaking is more accurate.

*

After that, it felt like there was a new era coming to the club, which was inevitable really. My contract had actually run out and there was a lot of change around the club. Frank Clark wanted me to stay and offered me a new deal but it just felt like the right time to go. I hadn't played much the season before and Derby felt like a fresh start. I had a young family and the move meant they wouldn't need to be uprooted.

Yeah, I know . . . *Derby.* I get it.

I wasn't a Midlands boy but I knew they were 'the enemy'. I understand the rivalry and if I'd been at West Ham looking at a move to Spurs, I'd have understood it even more.

But you have to do what you think is right. I didn't even know if I was going to be a regular at Forest, but I knew Arthur Cox was really keen on me and I thought I'd play regularly there, which I did.

It wasn't easy to go though; like I say, it was one big family at Forest and I was leaving a lot of good friends, but I thought it was the right thing to do. Although the fee was £750,000, money didn't come into it and it wasn't like I was jumping ship to stay in the Premier League because Derby were in the Championship too.

But I can understand the stick I got. Fans don't like it and I don't think anyone else made that move for about another 15 years!

Of course, football being football, where was my first away game for Derby? The City Ground. Whoever did the fixture list back then . . . thanks for that.

I took absolute pelters, got absolutely hammered by the fans with every touch. It's just the way it is, isn't it? They want their team to win and they want to put you off, but really, it doesn't have much effect. You just play the game.

It was 1-1 that night and I felt much worse in the reverse fixture when Forest won 2-0. I was at fault for the second goal as Steve Stone closed down a back-pass and it spun into the net.

*(What do you mean 'own goal'? It's Stoney's all day long!)*

Obviously Forest went up that year while Derby lost out in the play-offs, but I was genuinely pleased to see Forest promoted.

I had a lot of mates there and you don't spend that long somewhere without having feelings for the place.

After Derby, I went to Villa where I suffered a really bad ankle injury that I never really recovered from.

I was out for two years or so but eventually managed to get back and made a move out to Benfica under Graeme Souness, which was an unbelievable experience, before finishing my career by fulfilling an ambition to play for West Ham.

I still live up in Derbyshire and there's plenty of Forest fans around and I get on well with them. For every negative comment I get, there are 100 positive ones and I always want to see Forest do well.

I think most would say that I did quite well for them as a young lad who'd come through the ranks for free and, most importantly, I always gave 100 per cent every game.

The bottom line is, no-one can ever take my Forest memories away from me.

I'm proud to have represented them and I know I was extremely fortunate to play for the great Brian Clough and have him as my manager for eight years. I played with so many great players, appeared in cup finals, won caps for my country and made hundreds of appearances, so I achieved a lot for someone supposedly *'too small'*.

I know it should have been more. I've had issues in my life and football can be a cruel game - it takes a toll on your mind, body and soul.

I look back on my days with Forest with a smile on my face, though. It was the happiest time of my career and the best football education anyone could get.

Brian Clough used to say: 'Give everything you've got in every game, because it's a short career and you don't want to look back with any regrets.'

As ever, he was right. I don't think many people genuinely get through their careers - *or life* - with no regrets.

But if you can look in the mirror and say you gave it everything you had . . . *well, that's the Nottingham Forest way, young man.*

CHAPTER 10

# STEVE CHETTLE: THE TRENT END

The first time I ever went to see Forest play, I sat on my dad's shoulders in the old Trent End.

I'd have only been about seven and it would have been about 1976 in the old Second Division, just before Brian Clough came in.

*Blimey, I'm showing my age already, aren't I?*

In all honesty, I can't remember much about the game, which is a shame really, because it would have been the era of Ian Bowyer, Tony Woodcock, Peter Withe and big Larry Lloyd at the back - a great side.

What I do remember as a young lad was the excitement of it all; the walk up to the ground, seeing the stadium across the river, the noise, the singing, the smiles on all the grown-ups' faces.

It was infectious to a young lad like me.

I could tell there was something special about this place and, let's be honest . . . I wasn't wrong.

It was an old-fashioned football ground at the time; people smoking, standing up, corrugated roofs etc, but it had this aura about it.

It's changed a lot in the years since, but it's still got it.

Maybe it's the setting by the side of the Trent, but no matter much how the ground is developed, it's never lost that unique spirit.

When you're older and you look back, you remember all the drama that's taken place there, the glory nights, the wins, the great players, the ups and the downs and, for me personally, the over-riding feeling of being lucky enough to pull on that famous shirt.

It's just a great stadium, the City Ground, packed full of history and memories for everyone who goes there.

Like most people in Nottingham, Forest had always been my team and that was that. I guess I was lucky in that respect!

We'd won the FA Cup in 1959 but really, we'd been a decent team without having loads of success.

All that changed, of course, when Brian Clough arrived and achieved, well, miracles.

Those European nights were incredible. I was stood on the Bridgford End when Garry Birtles and Colin Barrett scored against Liverpool and remember that game well.

I was only nine, but what an atmosphere and the scenes when those goals went in. The city that night . . . well, just unbelievable.

The second leg a couple of weeks later at Anfield was on my tenth birthday so going through was probably the best present I could have asked for. *(Or maybe a Chopper!)*

To win the European Cup that year and then retain it - well . . . what a side, what a manager and what times we had.

How does it go? We had the whole world in our hands.

As for me, well I started out with the Nottingham Schools Under-11s . . . as a goalkeeper.

I was only nine when I was picked and it wasn't because I was the biggest kid in town, but probably because I could kick it the furthest.

They quickly decided I wasn't going to be a 'keeper but I did play a lot of positions when I was just starting out. A lot of my youth career was spent at left-wing and I scored quite a few goals from out there.

When I was 12, I signed for Notts County and also played for Parkhead and Padstow, which was a sort of Forest representative team around that time.

A couple of years later, Alan Hill left County and went across to Forest as head of recruitment so I followed him there.

I had a growth spurt when I was around 14 or 15, so of course, I ended up at centre-back which was my favourite position anyway, so thankfully it all worked out in the end.

I was also chuffed to have grown a few inches because we played Celtic around that time and I was right at the back of the Trent End - packed in like sardines that night too. But at least with my new-found height I could see the game as we enjoyed another memorable European run.

To say I was chuffed to be at Forest is an understatement - because it was a dream, really.

I was playing for the representative teams on a Sunday and also going in to train during the school holidays.

For me, it was fantastic, I was getting to see the likes of Ian Bowyer up close and understand just how good those guys were - real men, who had been there, done it and won it.

It was more running than anything else and while it was exciting, it was also scary to be around these people who had won European Cups and been legends of the game.

The biggest of them all and my favourite player as a kid? John Robertson, of course.

What a player, what a guy.

Physically . . . how can we put this? Everyone knows he may not have been the most typical footballer physique you'll ever see (!) but then there wasn't much typical about the skill and the ability he had either.

He could move the ball and beat someone with his first touch and put cross after cross in to the strikers, chance after chance on a plate. They must have loved playing with him, because it would just have been a string of perfect crosses, clever through balls, great goals from out wide - one of the all-time greats.

When I first got in and around Forest, I couldn't wait to meet him - being a Forest fan, it was a big thing for me.

*And the first time I came across him?* He was asleep under the snooker table in the social club where we used to eat our lunches.

So that was a great first impression - and, no, I didn't wake him up!

Some people might say 'never meet your heroes' but for me it was brilliant - that was probably par for the course with John. He was a one-off and nothing could dent him in my eyes.

Later on, I got to play with him in the reserves and it's something I'll always be grateful for. He was coming to the end of his career and obviously I was just starting out, but I will always be able to say: *'I played in the same team as John Robertson.'*

People might think I'm on about the European Cup days - if only! - but I'm not quite that old.

I was in and around the reserves and occasionally getting into to first team squad from a young age - 16 or 17 - and, of course, Brian Clough was still the manager.

He treated all us lads really well, both in a football sense and as young people. As apprentices, we did all the football work, but we also had to go over and do jobs for the gaffer.

We'd do his garden, walk his dog, paint his fences, do whatever - and he'd look after you like one of his own. He'd put the TV on, make lunch and talk to you about football or just life in general.

He taught you really good values; how to be polite, respectful, how to conduct yourself and it was just a really good upbringing, learning life skills as much as anything else, as well as getting a football education from one of the all-time greats.

*I look back now and realise just how lucky we were.*

Of course, we still had to do all the normal apprentice tasks; I used to clean the boots for people like Gary Mills, Garry Birtles and Johnny Metgod - who had huge feet, by the way.

They must have been size 12's, so it's no wonder he could strike a ball like he did.

I remember that goal against West Ham - *who doesn't?* - and he had such a great technique, but also so much power.

Now you know why; those size 12's - massive.

I used to get given boots from Paul Hart too; hand-me-downs, of course, never new boots.

The only time you'd get new boots from players was when they wanted them breaking in!

But I really enjoyed my two-year apprenticeship, I loved every minute of it in fact. I became a master at making cups of tea - that was my first job every morning, to take the first team's tea into the dressing room. I don't think you'd get that any more - times have changed a bit, these days, but for us, it was a proper grounding.

As for other lads who were around at that time, Phil Starbuck was coming through and got in the first team just before me, Lee Glover was a year younger, Terry Wilson made the first team, Gary Charles was a couple of years younger so there was a good crop of youngsters coming through.

The recruitment was sharp and the good thing about Forest was, they aren't afraid of giving youth a chance in the first team, pretty quickly.

It was possibly 'needs must' at the time, as there was no youth squad so anyone who wasn't playing in the first team was playing in the reserves.

And that was a good thing, as you got to play alongside professionals and against professionals, sometimes really experienced players and you had to quickly learn how to handle that.

You may have only been 17, but you had to adapt fast to cope with playing against men.

The other thing was, you saw how these experienced pros got out of situations, especially at the back - nudges, turns, little tricks of the trade you could pick up.

These days, development football plays it a bit safer in terms of the games. The facilities and pitches are a lot better, the quality is probably a bit better and the environment is a bit more shielded than we were.

There's a lot to be said for that, but the key question is how well it prepares young players for the 'real thing'.

Back then, reserve games were frenetic matches; there was a proper league, they were played in the stadiums, you'd get some fans turning up and you got a better preparation for what first team games were going to be like.

One of the games I remember is coming up against Kenny Burns who was coming to the end of his career up at Barnsley.

It was a real winter's night, freezing cold, the pitch was solid and he was wearing studs on a rock hard surface, no quarter given, as you can imagine - and a masterclass in defending from a Forest legend. They're the type of games you remember and that whole period was a really good learning curve.

In fact, it was so good I made my debut as an 18-year-old away at Chelsea. I came on in the second half and Brian Clough told me to 'play right wing like a centre back'.

It might sound odd, but it came with a clear instruction: win the ball and give it to someone who was better than me - which was everyone else in the team!

We lost 4-3 on the day and, to be honest, I don't remember a lot about the game.

It was at Stamford Bridge, but it didn't really look like it does now; there was the old Shed stand, a big running track around the pitch *(that I think they still had greyhound racing on)* and there were only 18,500 on.

All the glamour of the old First Division (!) but I took it in my stride, I think, and just loved the fact that I'd got onto the pitch.

Afterwards, Brian didn't give me a big de-brief or anything, which I soon learned was normal. He didn't say much after the games, really.

He was very motivational beforehand and had his snippets of wisdom during the game, but he was normally very quiet after the games, no matter what the result was.

I think he just trusted his players to know what they were doing, to understand the game as it was being played and to appreciate that they were representing this great club.

A couple of weeks later, Gary Fleming was unavailable through injury so on September 26, 1987 - a day before my 19th birthday - I made my full debut away at Norwich.

I played at right-back, a position I'd never really played before, but you just have to adjust accordingly - I'd have probably dusted off my gloves and played in goal if they'd asked me!

Norwich were a decent side and I think I might have been up against Dale Gordon on the day, but Neil Webb scored twice and we ran out 2-0 winners.

That night, as luck would have it, we were going away on one of our squad breaks to Majorca.

We used to go away three times a year to recharge our batteries - September, January and at the end of the season - because I think the gaffer had a place out there.

So that was a great way for a young lad to celebrate turning 19; make your full debut then jet off to Spain with Nottingham Forest for the weekend. Talk about living the dream.

I stayed in the team at right back for about the next six months after that game as the team finished third in the league. The only downside really was that there was no European football at the time as English clubs were still banned.

These days, of course, finishing third would get us in the Champions League with everything that comes with it. Who knows what we'd have gone on to achieve?

We also had a good run in the FA Cup, losing 2-1 to Liverpool in the semi-final, where I went on another steep learning curve.

We'd beat Liverpool a couple of weeks earlier at the City Ground and I'd done well against John Barnes, a fantastic player, probably the best in the country at that time.

The journalist John Sadler of The Sun was a friend of Brian's and asked if I'd do an interview in the build-up to the semi-final.

It was fairly straightforward stuff and the crux of it was: 'What's your ritual before a game?'

I just said 'beans on toast' but, of course, editorial licence and all that type of thing goes on and when the paper came out it became . . . *'I'll have Barnes on toast'.*

Well, you can imagine the fuss after that - over something I hadn't even said.

All the way to the stadium as our coach made its way to through Sheffield, all the Liverpool fans just had this plastered against windows of their buses, pointing at it, then pointing at me.

It was my first interview and I'd been done up like a kipper - on toast. Of course, come the game itself, who gets away from me? *John Barnes.* Who brings him down for a penalty? *Yours truly.*

We ended up losing 2-1 and I've had to live it with ever since - even though it's not something that I ever said.

But, hey, you live and learn and you've got to take it on the chin and move forward with a lesson learned the hard way: Pick your newspapers and pick the people that you speak to carefully.

On the plus side, we did get a trip to Wembley that year.

In April, there was the Football League Centenary Tournament - also known as the Mercantile Credit Football Festival. *(What do you mean, you don't remember that one?)*

It was an invitational tournament, with the likes of Forest, Everton, Aston Villa, Newcastle involved in playing games against each other at Wembley over one weekend. People may scratch their heads, but for us, if we were in a tournament, we wanted to win it.

I have to admit, it was a strange one though.

The games were only 40 minutes long, there was hardly anyone there and lots of the games went to penalties. We beat Sheffield Wednesday in the final in a shoot-out, so it's another one in the trophy cabinet at the City Ground somewhere, even if people have forgotten about it.

The thing is, it was being played over a weekend during the season so a couple of days later we were back in league action.

I'm not sure the Premier League would be up for that these days, but back then we went with the flow and I don't care what anyone says, I've got a winners medal to show for it.

*

I was in and around the England set-up around that time and that summer we jetted off for the Toulon Tournament in France with the Under-21s and I tell you what, looking back, we had a very good side.

There was me and Nigel Clough from Forest, Nigel Martyn in goal, Julian Dicks, Steve Redmond and Colin Cooper in defence.

In midfield we had Michael Thomas, David Platt, skipper David Rocastle and some Geordie lad called Paul Gascoigne, who could play a bit. David Thomas, of Coventry, partnered Nigel up top and Stuart Ripley, David Hirst and Vinny Samways were also around, so we were strong all over the pitch with players who all went on to have good careers.

We eventually lost 4-2 to France after extra time in the final - David Ginola scored for them - but it was a great experience and Dave Sexton was a fantastic coach to play under.

He was a bit unorthodox with his training at times; he'd get us practising slide tackles and diving headers, which was all a bit new to me, but he was great at getting the best out of people and having the team work hard.

Steve Redmond had come through at Manchester City and they always had a great youth system up there at that time; players like Paul Lake, David White and Ian Brightwell were getting a chance at a young age, just like we were in Nottingham.

The under-21s used to travel with these senior team and at at time, Forest had Stuart Pearce, Steve Hodge, Neil Webb, Des Walker, so there was a whole bunch of us lads flying the flag and they were always good trips.

I had the privilege of captaining my country against Albania and am proud of representing my country at that level.

People might ask if I'm disappointed not to have made the full squad later in my career, but not at all really - there were better players than me out there.

There was Terry Butcher, Mark Wright, Des was around and Tony Adams is one of my favourite players of all time, so I don't have any complaints at all. It was a golden era for English centre-halves and to have pulled on the jersey and get 12 caps as an Under-21 makes me very proud to this day.

*

The season after the Toulon Tournament, I was still in the team at right back and managed to score my first goal away at Norwich on the opening day, even though we lost 2-1. That season we had Lee

Chapman and Nigel Clough banging in the goals, with help from Stevie Hodge and Neil Webb in midfield. Steve gave you perpetual movement and Neil was the type of player who could just do everything.

Again, we had a good year and a highlight for me was getting my first goal at the City Ground in a 4-0 win over Charlton.

Me and Tommy Gaynor had come on for Lee Chapman and Garry Parker, but I don't know why or how I ended up in the box - other than it was the last minute and we were 3-0 up at the time.

When in went in, it was just a great feeling but to be honest, in terms of celebration, I didn't really know what to do.

That stuck with me throughout my career - I didn't get many so when it came to celebrating, it was just a look of surprise more than anything else: *'Blimey, I've scored!'*

We got to the League Cup final that year and that was really my first experience of being involved in a a big game at Wembley - I think the League Cup had a bit more importance back then and it was a bigger thing than maybe it is now.

I was only on the bench and didn't get on as we won 3-1, but it was great to be involved, get a medal and also a nice new suit.

Some clubs might have had deals with Burtons or wherever, but we were lucky that Paul Smith, the top designer, is from Nottingham and is a big Forest fan, so we were always well kitted out in top quality gear.

Sadly, I haven't kept any of them from down the years - they probably went to the local charity shop. If so, someone will have landed an absolute bargain there at some point.

That League Cup final was the start of a golden period of Wembley appearances for us, from the FA Cup through to some more obscure competitions.

To be fair, the League and the FA were trying to compensate for the lack of European games, but it still rankles that we weren't allowed to take on some of the top teams on the continent at a time when we had a really good side.

It would also have raised the profile of the club across Europe again and to miss out on playing those top class sides still hurts.

If nothing else, it would have given us more experience under our belts for later on when we did come back into the competitions a few years down the line.

Whatever happened that season though will always be overshadowed by the tragedy at Hillsborough.

Looking back, I was lucky in a way that I was on the bench that day, so I was spared the close-up reality of what was happening at the time.

Obviously, the game wasn't very long going when we saw a commotion in the Leppings Lane end and started to see people coming over the fences.

It quickly became apparent that the teams would have to come off the pitch and we were ushered into the dressing room, without really knowing what had happened or what was still happening at all.

My family were in the main stand at that end, so they could see the tragedy unfolding, but down in the dressing room, we were unaware.

An official from the FA came in and said we'd have to wait until they could clear the pitch but after about half an hour we heard that someone had died.

I don't think we could take it in at first - it seemed unreal. We were thinking: *'Crikey, how can someone have died at a football match?'*

It just didn't seem real. But as the minutes went by and the tragedy became clearer it was just, well, a mixture of terrible emotions, all absolutely heartbreaking.

They said they'd have to cancel the game but by that point, it had long since stopped being important.

We went up to the hospital in Sheffield and saw some of the people involved on the day and it was just so, so awful. It was just a huge tragedy and a terrible, tragic day.

The game was replayed at Old Trafford a few weeks later and I think that was the right thing to do.

I didn't play, but even though we were disappointed with the result, I think it was fitting that there was an all-Liverpool final that year with the reds winning the trophy after extra time.

*

Back in the league the following season, Brian Laws had made the right-back slot his own, with Pearcey on the other side, so I had to wait for opportunities a bit more, but when they came, they were largely down the middle, partnering Des Walker.

It's funny because these days, with the systems people play, you have a left-sided and a right-sided centre half.

We didn't really have that. I tended to play just in front of Des to attack the first ball with the striker and if anything came past, well, you'll never beat Des Walker.

He just mopped everything up and nine times out of ten he'd clear up any mess that you'd made, so it was a perfect partnership.

Of course, Stuart was there as well and we'd play in this little triangle at the back, which again was a fantastic learning curve; don't panic, play your way out of trouble if you can, but if you can't - get it clear. No messing.

Stuart was brilliant with me and all the young players, but he was also absolutely ruthless. He'd help you and pass things on all the time.

But he would also tear strips off you if you got something wrong, especially if you consistently made the same mistakes.

It was never anything personal. Just that standards had to be maintained.

He would let you have it with both barrels and you had to have a set of broad shoulders to cope with it, take it on board and learn from it.

Personally, we got on really well, we socialised with our wives and girlfriends and also as a pair, going out to concerts and things.

We went to Birmingham to see The Cure, Spear of Destiny a few times - just some great nights out.

You could let your hair down a bit more back then - nowadays there might be some video footage of us bopping about with our dance moves, which I'd dread to think about.

Thank God there were no mobile phones back then (!).

But I think that close relationship helped us on the pitch too and as a team, we always stuck together and stood up for each other. That was in-built in us at Forest.

We played good football, but we were no push-overs if teams wanted to mix it. Did I mention Stuart Pearce was captain?!

We finished ninth that season, with Stevie Hodge as our top scorer on 14 goals in all competitions.

Hodgey had that great ability to see when Nigel had dropped into midfield so would get on a run to go past him and find space where Nigel could then thread the ball through the eye of a needle to find him.

The club also brought in Nigel Jemson as a new striker around Christmas time and it was a move that paid off later on.

He was only 18 when he came down and he moved in round the corner from me and my girlfriend (now my wife), so we took him under our wing a bit and made sure he was looked after in this big new city.

He's still a mate of mine and a real character, Nigel. He doesn't mention the League Cup final that year every day . . . *just most days!*

It was another great occasion; glorious sunshine and a classic Forest side of that era; Garry Parker in midfield with Gary Crosby and Franz Carr down the wings and Nigel and Jemmo up front.

They had a good side too with the likes of Denis Irwin and Earl Barrett. I was up against Andy Ritchie, who was a really good player and Roger Palmer, another clever centre forward from that time, but I really enjoyed the game.

Steve Sutton made a great fingertip save towards the end to keep it 1-0 and getting a clean sheet and the trophy made it a thoroughly enjoyable day.

*Can't remember who scored for us though . . !*

We came straight back to Nottingham afterwards but there wasn't a big night out or anything. We had a civic reception in the square, which was absolutely great, but I don't really remember us having a big do or anything.

We just got on with it and don't forget, we still had a couple of league games left.

Despite winning the League Cup, Brian Clough called us *'failures'* for our league form but if that was a motivational technique, it all came together against Manchester United in our next home game.

We were three up inside half an hour when Jemmo tried an outrageous overhead kick from the edge of the box.

It came back off the bar and I managed to nod it home to put us 4-0 up at half-time and that's the way it stayed with the Trent End absolutely bouncing for the rest of the game.

Maybe it was payback for the FA Cup tie earlier that season when Mark Robins had scored to knock us out 1-0 and - *allegedly* - save Sir Alex Ferguson from the sack. Just think what a mistake that would have been at Old Trafford.

For me personally, the following season was really memorable. I played 37 out of 38 league games - only missing Everton away because I had a dead leg, a fact that still bugs me even now.

For the first few years, I hadn't really nailed down a position in the team; I'd played left back at times, filled in at right back and sometimes down the middle.

But from 1991, I had a really good partnership with Des and me in the middle, Stuart at left-back and mainly Brian Laws down the right.

Mark Crossley had made the goalkeeper position his own and was a phenomenal keeper, as well as being a great character in the dressing room. What can you say about Norm? He's just a one-off.

Me? I wasn't the most skilful player in the world, but I had a decent left foot, could head the ball pretty well and people might say I was tough in the tackle.

Mainly, I tried to keep the game simple. I knew my role in the team was to try to break stuff up and try to help spring counter attacks.

We sat pretty deep as a team and played counter-attacking football, breaking on people with the pace that we had in midfield, especially.

Even at the City Ground we'd sit in, with Nigel dropping deep to collect it and having wide players going past him.

The thing with doing that is you have to be able to play - and we could do that. We could play our way out of trouble, we could beat 'blocks', as they call them today, and we played good attacking football.

People might talk about that as a Brian Clough philosophy, but really he was just adamant that the game was simple.

We didn't do any analysis of the opposition, we didn't do any analysis of our own performances.

He just said: '*If you can play, you can play. If you can't play, you wouldn't be here. So let's go out and play some football.*'

He just wanted you to go out, enjoy yourself and play the game as it should be played. It was almost the definition of 'simple, but effective', because it worked so well for us.

There wasn't a big presentation on the opposition before games; there was nothing on a noticeboard showing their strengths and weaknesses or whatever.

We didn't get bombarded with statistics and information, there was no video bank of games and clips for us to study - it was a case of watching Match of the Day and seeing who was doing what.

As players, we would look at our opponents individually and obviously, you'd think back to games you'd had against them in the past, where they'd done a little trick, or you knew which side they liked to get on. But really we'd look at our own game, we always spoke about what we were going to do as a group.

In training, we just played five-a-sides, every day. OK, it wasn't the most technical approach, but they were good for us.

You were in tight areas, looking to solve problems with not much space to work in, getting close, helping each other out, showing for passes, getting your head up to see what's around you - all with hardly any time because the pitches were so small.

In many ways, it was of its time, but also ahead of its time.

Brian often recruited small, skilful footballers who could find solutions to problems and get out of tight situations.

It's not dissimilar to Pep Guardiola's outlook now, with players like Raheem Sterling and David Silva; players with that quick, natural intelligence who can beat opponents in the blink of an eye.

That was the approach we had back then too, which helped me, as it was easy for me to find someone like Garry Parker or Gary Crosby who could really get at teams, with their pace, passing and quick feet.

Of course, there was another young player who had come to us that season and was about to make a bit of a name for himself.

Roy Keane was a lad from Cobh who had been around the reserves at the start of that 1990/91 season.

We'd drawn 1-1 with QPR at home on the opening Saturday and Roy had played for the reserves on the Monday night as a sub.

On the Tuesday, we were away at Liverpool and Brian used to like to bring some of the younger lads along, to give them some experience of what these games were like. They'd help the kit man, do odds and sods, just be around the place, see what it was like.

And I think that's what it was with Roy that night; we didn't know who this kid was at first, getting on the bus with his boots in a little bag.

I don't think he expected to play himself, but suddenly there he was, up against that classic Liverpool team in front of 30-odd thousand fans - like a duck to water. Not fazed at all, shouting, wanting the ball, like he was always meant to be there.

In training, he wasn't quite as loud as he became later on, but he wasn't respectful either.

He came from a boxing family in Ireland and he had no airs or graces; he just wanted to play football - and he wanted to win.

Roy didn't care who you were, who was established in the team, who had won what, who had authority or what the hierarchy was . . . he just wanted to win.

Well, we all wanted to win, but performances dictated whether you were going to be accepted into the group or not - and he stood out a mile. He just strolled through games.

He could play in any position and do everything - one of THE great players to play in the Premier League.

Now I'm a manager and coach, I look at games differently and when I watch some of the Forest games from then back, I can see how intelligent Roy was even as a young lad. His runs from deep and the timing of them were just spot on. He knew how to find those pockets of space at just the right time and get a shot off.

It seems obvious now, but Roy wasn't backwards in coming forwards, would you believe?

*If he had something to say, he'd say it. To anyone. He's not changed, has he?*

He's still the same person he was when he was a kid with us and no-one knew his name. He has opinions does Roy, and he lets you know what they are. You may have noticed this!

Back then at Forest, I think he was in the right place at the right time with the right club and the right manager.

One of Brian Clough's biggest principles was to get the ball, give it and move. That's what Roy was built for and I think the gaffer loved him. Yes, they had fiery moments every now and then - Brian Clough and Roy Keane? *Blimey. You can imagine.*

But it always settled down and they had huge respect for each other - Roy still names him as the best manager he played under to this day.

It helped having strong characters like that around the dressing room, but he was one of many. Me? Largely I went into my own zone before games anyway.

I was just concentrating on what I had to do, rather than worry about anyone else's opinions about the bigger picture maybe.

Because there were some really top opponents out there and you had to be completely focused every game to do your job properly.

I remember Mark Hughes was a really tough competitor; he was like a bull, so strong and yet so skilful. He could do everything, if you gave him an inch.

I also never used to like playing against Niall Quinn, who was a lot better than people give him credit for with his feet, as well as being a real handful in the air.

Ian Rush was still about, Graeme Sharp at Everton was a nightmare to play against and Tony Cottee was always hard to pick up; there were so many top strikers around in that era, you could go on and on about it.

Most teams had a top-class centre forward who would get around 20 goals a year and it says a lot that so many of them are still big names in the game even now, nearly 30 years on.

We improved slightly on the previous season in the league, finishing eighth as Arsenal won the title.

I managed to score probably my best goal that season, leathering one in from outside the box at the Trent End against Sunderland after Nigel laid it off to me. It just sat up perfectly and flew into the top corner - a great feeling for a Nottingham lad to score a goal like that at the Trent End.

We finished with a bit of a flourish, beating Derby at home *(which is always nice isn't it?)*, then scoring 12 goals in two games over four days at the City Ground.

First we beat Chelsea 7-0, when Ian Woan got his first goal for the club, and then we beat Norwich 5-0 with Woany on the scoresheet again.

We then drew with Tottenham and beat Liverpool 2-1 *(with another goal from this Ian Woan lad!)*, before seeing off Leeds 4-3 on the last day of the league season.

But the game that everyone probably remembers most from that year is the FA Cup Final.

*

We'd had some ding-dong games against Crystal Palace in the earlier rounds and it was a long campaign for us to get to Wembley - a real slog. It was the biggest game of my career but the attitude from Brian and the coaching staff was 'it's just another game'.

Among ourselves though, we were all saying: *'Hey, come on - we need to win this for the gaffer.'*

We were absolutely determined to give him the trophy that had eluded him so far, especially as the press kept on about it every year.

Archie Gemmill and Liam O'Kane might have passed on some words of advice before the game, but the gaffer ruled the dressing room and it was a very quiet place normally.

This was before the days of ghetto-blasters and pumping each other up with loud music and whatnot.

It was just . . . quiet and calm.

We had a ball on a towel in the middle of the dressing room and everyone had to sit round, relax, put their feet out and the gaffer would just point to the football and say: *'That's what we play with lads - go out there and look after it.'*

That was about as technical as it got - and this was the FA Cup Final.

These were the days when the whole country stopped to see the game - obviously, it's still big now, but back then it was absolutely huge.

Glorious sunny day again (as it always seemed to be), the old Wembley absolutely packed, the marching band, the twin towers, the gaffer wearing his 'World's Best Grandad' badge and Prince Charles and Diana as guests of honour.

I don't normally get starstruck or anything and at the time it was just par for the course, but when I look back now and people mention Princess Diana, I say: *'Oh yes, I met her once . . .'*

We didn't have a conversation or anything just 'hello' 'good luck' and whatnot, but it's all part of the occasion.

Obviously, what most people outside Forest remember that final for is Gazza getting injured.

But for me, he shouldn't have been on the pitch to even make that tackle.

I knew Paul from the Under-21s and you could see he was all hyped up and excited beforehand, but the challenge on Garry Parker early on is a straight leg to the chest - horrendous.

In any walk of life, let alone football, that's assault and he should have gone right there and then.

The referee Roger Milford, admitted afterwards that he should have sent Paul off and you wonder what might have been if he had done.

Gazza wouldn't have got injured and his career might have gone in a different direction.

The crazy thing is, he didn't even get booked for that first challenge. Even a yellow might have calmed him down and made him think twice about the tackle on Gary Charles.

But instead, he flew into that one and did his knee. Again, an atrocious tackle and, let's be frank, Gary was lucky not to be injured too.

Stuart scored from the free-kick with a goal that absolutely leathered into the top corner.

It was one of THE great Cup Final goals and although I've never claimed the 'assist', me and Lee Glover were in the wall and our job was to move the last player to make room for the shot.

We'd lean in and pull and tug and roll the opponent to get him out of the way - although to be fair, when they saw that shot coming in, they would probably have ducked anyway (!). I'm not sure what VAR would have made of our wall shenanigans these days, mind.

There was also a Gary Lineker goal that was ruled out for offside that was well onside as well, so thank goodness for no video checks back then.

We must have been convincing with our appeals: *'He's miles off, referee!'*

Of course, you don't know if he was or not, but you've got to ask the question (and I've always had an honest face!).

We'd scored quite early and hung on to half-time, with Norm saving a Lineker penalty, so at that point, it looked like we might do it.

We were a good side, but we were up against a good side too; they had Lineker, Paul Stewart, Vinny Samways was a good technician and funnily enough when Gascoigne went off, it probably cost us.

I think if he'd stayed on, the game might have passed him by, especially once he'd been yellow carded, but they brought Nayim on instead, who was another really skilful player and he made a bit of a difference.

What should have happened is they'd have gone down to 10 men, but of course that didn't happen.

That's football isn't it? Huge things can hang on one decision and that day, that one went against us.

Lo and behold, Paul Stewart got the equaliser and it went to extra time. Some people have made a thing about the gaffer not coming over to talk to us after 90 minutes. He stayed on the bench, but in all honesty, it didn't affect us.

It was par for the course with Brian. I don't think he would have tried to change anything tactically and I think it was a sign that he trusted us to know what to do.

We had to perform and solve the problems ourselves, we didn't need the manager to tell us that, so it wasn't a big issue for him to leave us to it before that extra time started.

Terry Venables was probably the other way; issuing all sorts of instructions, but it wasn't tactics that decided the game, it was a fluke header that came off Des.

There was nothing he could do about that, it was just one of those things in a really tight game that sometimes goes against you.

Losing was hard and disappointing, but that's football. You can't cry about it, you've just got to get your head up and go again next time.

If we had won, it would probably have been the right time for Brian to bow out at that stage, having got the lot.

But it wasn't to be, so we dusted ourselves down, had a few weeks off and then got back at it.

*

We hadn't really scored enough goals and the club looked to change that by bringing in Teddy Sheringham from Millwall for £2 million.

Teddy was a great player and the only thing wrong with his time at Forest is that it wasn't long enough.

We still had Nigel up front, who was as consistent as ever, but Jemmo left for Sheffield Wednesday in September.

We still had a good side, but the league was getting tougher.

Teams were starting to invest a lot more and the standard was going up each year. Players were fitter, things were getting more tactical, people were stepping up their preparation for games.

Things were definitely starting to change, but we were still doing what we'd always done. The game was evolving and we weren't really evolving quick enough.

We still had the basis of a good side and adding people like Teddy helped, but all it was doing really was keeping us where we were - around eighth or ninth - and the top teams were starting to pull away a bit.

It was the last season of the old First Division before the Premier League era began and we did OK, but it got harder and harder.

Scotty Gemmill came in and gave us extra energy in midfield - he could run all day, couldn't he? - and Carl Tiler was around by then, which was good for us, as Des had a spell out injured and I missed virtually the entire second half of the season through injury too.

And after making 54 appearances the previous season, I managed only 23 league games and that was always hard to take.

It meant I missed out on another Wembley final, when we lost 1-0 to Man United in the League Cup again.

I travelled down to the game, but wasn't involved due to the injury, so that was a disappointing day all round.

I was on the bench for the last-ever Zenith Data Systems Cup Final *(the big one)* against Southampton that year, coming on for Pearcey at left-back.

It was a good game actually, Scotty Gemmill scored a great volley and Kingsley Black made it two before they got back into it - Matt Le Tissier of all people scored a header and then they made it 2-2.

But Scotty grabbed the winner in extra time with another good finish towards the end, so it was another trophy and a good day out for the fans, because don't forget there was about 70,000 there.

People might turn their noses up, but like I've said, for us it was one of those things where if you're in a competition, you're in it to win it and it was a golden period for Forest to go to so many games down there.

You don't go out thinking *'oh this cup's not so important, so I won't track my man'* - you give it your best effort, same as every other game.

One of the other games people remember from that last season before it became the Premier League was us beating Notts County 4-0 at Meadow Lane.

They were relegated that year, so missed out on all the new approach, money, etc and some people might ask if I had mixed feelings about it.

*Nope. Not at all.*

We played really well that day; Gary Crosby and Gary Charles scored, Teddy got one and Roy went on anther one of his runs from deep for the fourth.

Notts County were a big First Division club at the time and it's got worse and worse as the years have gone by. I've spent time there myself in recent years so I know the history of the club. But the relationship between us and them back in the 1990s was really weird.

The shy and retiring Neil Warnock was the manager at the time and we'd have proper eleven-a-sides against each other on a Friday morning.

We both had games on the Saturday - but even so, those Friday games were brutal.

Our training grounds were literally a row of trees apart and the coaching staff used to just let us get on with it, so some of the challenges and things that went on were horrendous.

No holding back, proper challenges flying in and then you might have to patch yourselves up for a First Division game the next day.

It would never happen now in a million years, but I think both managers loved it at the time.

I've got a lot of time for Neil, he does what he does and he does it well, because he's successful everywhere he goes.

County went down that year and we finished a solid eighth, so there was no obvious indication that we might be in trouble the following year as this bright and shiny new Premier League dawned.

Des left for Sampdoria, where I don't think they ever knew where to use him properly, but Carl was still there and we'd played well together on many occasions.

*One thing that probably goes unmentioned is that the rules changed and the back pass to goalkeepers was outlawed, so that was quite a significant thing for a back four to get to grips with.*

Teddy scored a great goal - the first on TV in the new era - as we beat Liverpool in our opening game and we looked well set at that point. I thought we were going to have a right go.

I remember Norm saying: *'D'you know what lads? I fancy us to do something special this year . . .'*

But, as everyone now knows, it just didn't happen and things unravelled from there.

Teddy went to Spurs after just three games, we didn't keep enough clean sheets, we didn't score enough goals, other teams were evolving and we just didn't keep pace.

It's brutal and it's painful, but it's as simple as that really.

On paper, you look at the squad and the team that we had and we should have been good enough to stay up, but . . .

It wasn't through lack of effort and there was no big fracture in the dressing room. We didn't lose heart.

We seemed to lose a lot of games by the odd goal, I can't remember us getting hammered too often and even right towards the end, we were still going to Arsenal and getting a draw.

We beat the likes of Chelsea and Spurs, but overall . . . it wasn't enough.

We could all see the gaffer wasn't in the best of health and we could see that getting progressively worse, but every man was giving everything they had for him, for the team, for the fans and for the club.

It was just heartbreaking. Anyone who thinks players don't care should have been in that dressing room and seen the state of us.

Obviously the Sheffield United game was the last act, but we were always behind the eight ball all season, struggling throughout really.

But when it's mathematically done . . . it was just a sickening feeling for so many reasons.

We knew it would be the manager's last game at the City Ground and he deserved better than that season.

It was weird though because obviously we'd been relegated, but the fans were on the pitch cheering the manager's name. You wouldn't have had that anywhere else in the game, anywhere in the world.

All the way through the game, they'd been chanting 'Brian Clough' and there were banners, special scarves, everything.

It was so, so strange; there was this huge feeling of celebration for what the gaffer had achieved, mixed with sadness, not just about going down, but seeing this end of an era taking place.

It was the teams that he'd made that had put the club on the map really, the history that he'd created, the trophies he'd won.

We lost 2-0 on the day and that sort of summed things up.

*Brian Cough's time ended on a real low, which was unjust for someone of his stature not just in the club, but the game itself.*

He deserved better, but it wasn't for the want of trying with that group of players. There was no big farewell speech after the game, it wasn't the type of thing he would do.

But inside the dressing room that day, I was just in lockdown anyway about the reality of being relegated.

Amid everything else that was happening with Brian, we had to face up to the fact that the club had gone down and we'd been the players that season it happened.

*

It felt like a watershed moment where we needed to draw breath and start to put things right on the pitch under a new man - Frank Clark.

Obviously, he had great Forest heritage, he was hugely respected in the game and I think he saw the areas where we needed to change and to modernise.

We were now in Football League Division One, as it was called at the time, a step down from the Premier League.

We lost Roy Keane to Man United and Nigel went to Liverpool, but Pearcey stayed with us at a time when he was still an England regular - again, I'm not sure many players these days would do that, but it showed the feeling Stuart had for the club.

Gary Charles left, but Des Lyttle came in, as well as Colin Cooper, and those two lads proved to be fantastic signings for us.

I'd played with Colin with the Under-21s so we went back a long way and I knew how good he'd be.

Off the pitch, our young families grew up together as they were similar ages and I'm still really good mates with Colin, who works for the Chinese FA these days.

It felt like a renewal of the squad without throwing the baby out with the bathwater, and we were all looking forward to the season ahead.

One of the first things Frank did was bring a fitness coach in, a chap called Pete Edwards.

*First things first - we didn't know what the hell a fitness coach did!*

He was a little bit astounded when we reported back for pre-season. Everything that he had planned, he had to scale back by about fifty per cent when he saw us.

It was a matter of building up a new fitness regime that other clubs probably had a two-year start on us with.

In terms of diet, we'd been left to look after ourselves up to that point. We ate together on Friday nights before away games - these days a lot of clubs do that before home games, too, but back then we didn't do that.

But without a doubt when Pete came in, our fitness improved and we started to take things on a bit more about the right things to eat and how to look after ourselves properly.

Looking back, it's not rocket science, but it was just a way we had to start to move with the times a bit more and if it made us better players, everyone was all for it.

We were determined to get Forest back into the top league and Frank set about bringing in some new players to help us do that - none more so than Stan Collymore.

What a player Stan was - I'm on record saying he's the best I ever played with and I stand by that.

I liken him to the original 'R9' Ronaldo and I think if Stan hadn't had the problems that he had off the pitch at times, he would have been a major, major goalscorer for England.

He was quick, strong, decent in the air and had a hell of a shot on him. His tight control was top quality and, like all players with that much talent, they're a defender's nightmare because you never know what they're going to do next.

You could safely say that about Stan.

Dave Phillips also came in that summer to give us guile and experience and he was another great addition to the squad.

That season, we seemed to get better the longer it went on. Colin and I formed a great partnership at the back and whenever he went up front it was like he was a magnet for the ball, scoring seven or eight goals nearly every year.

He was a really tidy footballer who could play in midfield if required, too.

Not that we needed him there much that season; Steve Stone had really shown his quality there and we had the likes of Phillo, Scotty Gemmill and Ian Woan there still, so we were well stocked in midfield.

Lars Bohinen joined in November and Alf-Inge Haaland joined later on too, so the signings we were making were spot on.

Stan was banging the goals in up front and it was just a fantastic season to be a part of - I managed to play all 46 games in the league (no dead legs this time!) and it was a total contrast to the year before.

As a manager, Frank was more of a student of the game than Brian, who had his ways of how he wanted things done.

But Frank was more of a thinker and he'd do more work with us on the training ground, not just in terms of what we could do, but what the opposition were likely to do also.

It helped us catch up with the way the game was going pretty quickly, while at the same time making sure that we played to our strengths.

Quite often that involved just getting the ball up to Stan as quickly as possible, but quite often it led to a really good goal.

You only have to look at the Peterborough game, when we had to win to go up to see how important he was.

That day, beautiful sunshine, massive Forest following, all set up for us - and we were 2-0 down after ten minutes. *Football, eh?*

Top against bottom, but it was a tough, tough game.

Stan got us back into it before half-time, Stuart levelled it up with a typically brave diving header, but the winner from Stan . . . well, have a look at it on YouTube or whatever. What a goal - an absolute screamer. Left foot, on the charge, at an angle, top corner.

We took so many people down there that day and I've seen photos of fans up the floodlights and everything trying to get a view of the game and in the end it was a great, great occasion.

The scenes of the Forest fans celebrating at the end were just fantastic, it felt like we'd made up for being relegated - well, partially, at least.

They'd stuck with us after relegation and I do think the Forest fans are a special bunch.

I think every club has a proportion of supporters who will let you know what they think when things aren't going well *(!)* but that number at Forest is very, very small in my experience.

You look at the attendances, even when they went down to League 1 level and the fans stuck with them.

At the moment things are going well again in the Championship and the gates are always more than 20,000 (when fans are allowed in), while the away support is always a massive credit to the club.

They've seen some tough times now for the past 10 years, maybe more, and it's a Premier League club in everything but name.

They deserve success for their loyalty and - *fingers crossed* - that return to the top tier isn't far away now.

We managed it back in 1994 and enjoyed some great celebrations around the city at the time.

Maybe it had taken a relegation and then promotion straight away to get us back on an upward trajectory because we certainly came into the Premiership confident about what we could achieve.

*

Bryan Roy came in and what a character he was, as well as being a fantastic player; quick, nimble, great feet, good crosser and a top finisher. It was a bit of a gamble I think, as Frank spent a lot of the budget on Bryan, but he gave us that extra quality and formed a great partnership up front with Stan in that first season.

We'd seen him in the USA World Cup and he was a great fit with the club and the city.

Bryan integrated himself with the group really well and I know he still loves Nottingham; it's a great place for someone to come to - really friendly and people just take you to their hearts if you do well for them.

We had momentum and I think we went the first 11 games unbeaten in the league and there were some real highlights for us that year; beating Spurs 4-1 at their place and beating Man United 2-1 at Old Trafford.

They had an incredible side at that time, Giggs, Keane, Cantona, etc. Again, when people ask about toughest opponents, Cantona has to be right up there, bags of skill, incredible control and full of tricks and flicks.

Stan scored another screamer early on, before Stuart got a second. Cantona got one back and you could feel this wave after wave of United attacks coming at us. It was like the Alamo, but we managed to hold on and win the game - which I think was their only home defeat of the season.

We were really proud to have gone there and won, but when you get a result like that, there's no sign of the opposition manager.

Fergie would have been absolutely chewing - he probably spoke with the gaffer, but he wouldn't have wanted to come and see this *'little'* Nottingham Forest team who've just been promoted and now turned over his big hitters in their own back yard. No way.

We were playing without fear that season and getting some top results - we beat Sheffield Wednesday 7-1 at Hillsborough and I think that's still one of the biggest-ever Premier League away wins.

They had Des at the back by then, Chris Waddle, John Sheridan, some really good players - so to go there and take them apart like we did was just incredible.

We'd got good players, good spirit and a tactically astute manager - but the main attribute was probably having people who could score goals.

Stan could aways get us something out of nothing if the chips were down and behind him we had Woany, Stevie Stone and lads like Lars, who was naturally unbelievably fit, but also had great technical ability and would also chip in with some great goals and assists.

We finished third in the league and that's still the highest any promoted team has ever achieved in the Premier League - to be honest, I can't see anyone ever doing that again now.

The great news for us was that it got Forest back in European competition and the following season, we had some great nights in a very strong UEFA Cup that year.

Unfortunately, we were going to be without Stan, which was a massive blow. The fact that he was going to Liverpool for a record fee didn't make it any easier to swallow, but to be fair, the club did try to replace him.

We went away pre-season to Italy and we were shown a video of this guy playing for Torino who looked fantastic.

He'd played with Diego Maradona at Napoli and had all the attributes; big, quick, skilful.

Andrea Silenzi was the fella's name, but we didn't realise that the video was two years old.

And the Andrea Silenzi we signed was *not* the lad who was on those videos.

Bless him, he was a lovely chap - one of the nicest fellas you could ever meet - and he'd try his heart out . . . but it just didn't happen for him.

He had ability and he could play, but we'd watch him doing these overhead kicks and things in training and be thinking: *'Good luck with that in an English game!'*

I think he got two goals for us in cup games, but if anything could have gone wrong for him, it did - and I felt sorry for the lad.

He was the first Italian to play in the Premier League and there was no real support network for him, like they'd have now.

I think he came in because Kevin Campbell, who'd also come in, had got injured just before the start of the season. Kev was a great player, knew the league and would work hard for the team every game as well.

With Bryan still up there and Jason Lee around as well, we had decent options.

Chris Bart-Williams came in and was another good signing, so the club was well set again and it felt like we'd re-established ourselves in the Premier League that season.

What people are most likely to remember though is the UEFA Cup campaign and it was great to be part of a Forest team back in European action that season.

It was really, really tough, but a great experience.

What people probably don't realise when you look back is how many good sides were in the competition that year.

It was a time when the Champions League was still basically for the champions only, so some very good sides were taking part in the UEFA Cup. AC Milan with George Weah were in there, Barcelona with Luis Figo, PSV Eindhoven with the original Ronaldo, obviously Bayern with Klinsmann . . . and us.

So there was some top, top sides in that competition and I loved every minute of it.

First up were Malmo, where the pitch wasn't great, it was bitterly cold, but we grabbed an away goal in a 2-1 defeat so only needed one goal at the City Ground.

We banged on the door as they say and you could feel the pressure building up on their goal.

Eventually, a bit Route One, but Bryan got on the end of a wayward knockdown and fired a belter of a shot into the top corner on the run.

The place just went crazy and it was a hell of a goal to take us through.

The atmosphere that night was just unbelievable and people still talk to me about it now.

Against Auxerre, well . . . we got battered for two games, but managed to keep two clean sheets.

If you look at some of the players they had, half that team went on to be big, big names; Laurent Blanc, Taribo West, Stephan Guivarch, Lilian Laslandes and a lad in midfield called Sabri Lamouchi.

When he took over at Forest, someone asked me where I'd seen him before and I hadn't got a clue. Then you looked at that Auxerre team again and there he was. And I tell you what, they were no mugs.

They were two really tough games against them and again we did well to get past them.

Against Lyon it was Paul McGregor who put us ahead after that rarest of things - a Stuart Pearce penalty saved.

Macca nipped in for the rebound and it was like the football gods were smiling on us. I love Paul, he's a great lad and another one-off character. I've done the Reservoir Red Dogs podcast with him and he's not changed to this day - still the rockstar in the making.

I went to see his band Merc a couple of times and they were really good shows.

One time at Rock City and another at a pub called The Aviary just over Trent Bridge where he had a 'diva' strop like Liam Gallagher where he dropped his microphone and tried to smash the drums up because something went wrong. *He's a proper princess is Macca!*

Sharp as a tack as a footballer though, quick, brave and a real live wire, so it was no surprise he got in first for that rebound.

We went to Lyon and it was freezing - *deep snow on the ground* - but again we defended for our lives, backs to the wall for most of the game again, but we came out with the draw we needed.

What I remember about that night is Stuart Pearce giving us the equivalent of an English 'Braveheart' speech in the tunnel while both teams were lined up waiting to come out.

It was proper *'we will win this because we're effin' English!'* stuff.

The sight of a full-on Stuart Pearce, pumping us all up in his short-sleeved shirt, while most of their lads were in long sleeves and gloves.

They must have been thinking: 'What the hell is this?'

Ninety minutes later, they had their answer and we had the result that set us up for Bayern Munich.

One of the greatest sides in the world, in one of the most iconic stadiums, packed to the rafters with World Cup winners, megastars, us - and thousands of Forest fans who'd made the trip and never stopped singing all night. Fantastic support.

Jurgen Klinsmann scored for them after about a quarter of an hour and you could see maybe they thought this was going to be easy - after all they were used to steamrollering teams in Germany and beyond.

But then we got a free-kick almost straight away, just towards the left hand side of their box.

We had a routine we'd worked on where the ball gets played in by Phillo and I head it back across goal from beyond the far post for someone to nod in. I wasn't supposed to score - just get it back across goal.

At the time, as the ball came in, I didn't realise how far it had come - because I was virtually off the pitch when I got my head to it and all I was trying to do was get it back into the six-yard box.

It looked like it was going too far and the keeper Oliver Kahn got underneath it, so with the trajectory I just managed to get my head on it, hoping someone in the middle would nod it over the line.

And then - *bang* - it goes in. 1-1. An away goal. Unbelievable.

Silence everywhere . . . apart from the away section where the fans were going crazy.

Funnily enough, I always remembered watching Forest win the European Cup against Malmo and that was the same stadium, same end and same shot-put circle as where Trevor Francis scored.

And now me.

So yes, I was back to that *'delighted but surprised'* celebration.

If you watch it back, you can probably see that on my face!

The lads piled on and I didn't know what to do - but believe me, I was absolutely flying inside.

My wife was back home, pregnant at the time with one of our kids and she was lying down with a touch of sickness when she saw it on TV - she didn't know what to do either! She was like: *'Oh my God, he's scored!'*

It was just a great feeling and even though we ended up losing 2-1 on the night, the way that we'd played in Europe that season, we fancied our chances in the return leg.

Everywhere we'd been, we'd been battered away from home, but managed to grind out results and then go through back at the City Ground.

We stayed in games and with a 2-1 deficit, we knew that a 1-0 win in Nottingham would see us through. This though was our toughest test, for sure. They had a frightening team on paper; Klinsmann, Kahn, Christian Ziege, Lothar Matthaus - some of the top players in the world, but we were still confident.

We thought we'd gone 1-0 up when Colin Cooper scored, but it was disallowed for some reason. Either way, with the City Ground bouncing, we were going toe-to-toe with them. No holding back.

But then, ahhh . . .

It was almost half-time when they got a free-kick, Ziege hit it well and Norm has dived over it, which was massively unlike him, because he was so consistent for us.

That made it 3-1 on aggregate and, of course, gave them an away goal, too. The biggest problem we had then was that we had to go and chase the game.

And once we were doing that, they picked us off with the extra space that was around, Klinsmann got a hat-trick and it looks like they slaughtered us. But sometimes scorelines don't tell the full story and it was a close game for long periods.

We'd done well out of the away goal rule up to that point, but when it goes against you, it makes things really difficult.

They went on to win the trophy so there was no disgrace in losing to them, but it was still disappointing, even though we could hold our heads up high.

We ended up finishing ninth in the league that year and we were never lower than tenth, so there was no indication that things were going to go so wrong the following year.

But, as everyone knows, it did and the whole season was messy, really.

We started off with a 3-0 win away at Coventry when Kev Campbell got a hat-trick.

After the game, Mark Crossley said: 'You know what lads? I really fancy us to do well this season.'

*The kiss of death. Again. I blame Norm!*

That was the second time he'd said that and both times we got relegated. I love Mark to bits and he's a really funny guy as well as being absolutely lovely. He probably doesn't realise how funny he is half the time. Let's put it this way, he wouldn't have been top of the class at anything in school - other than goalkeeping.

I've heard him do his bits on podcasts and stuff and all I'll say is that there's an element of truth in everything he says. How big an element is a different matter though!

So with Norm's prediction ringing in our ears we had to wait until late December for our next win.

By then, Frank had gone and I still think that was the wrong move.

I'll always be grateful to Brian Clough for giving me the opportunity to play, but I really enjoyed it under Frank and he put together a really good side.

It was a knee-jerk reaction to lose him and I think given time he would have steadied the ship.

We'll never know, but I think it was unjust on him, given what he'd achieved in the space of two seasons.

It was a travesty really and then to put the pressure on one of the players - Stuart - to try to keep the club in the Premier League, when he had no experience of management was a very big ask.

I think when you look at it like that, you can see why things went awry that season.

But the bottom line is, we weren't good enough that year to stay up.

It's not a season that I can remember too much about if I'm honest. Maybe I've wiped it from my memory because it was all too painful.

I know we drew a lot of games and I think that shows how close the line is between success and failure.

Dave Bassett came in to help Stuart towards the end and we brought Pierre Van Hooijdonk in, but I think we only won one game from February onwards and that's obviously nowhere near good enough.

We had to take it on the chin.

I don't think we ever thought we were too good to go down. We spent most of the season at the wrong end of the table, so it wasn't like we dropped in there right at the end.

But it just didn't go for us, despite us having a good squad on paper that had done well in the past.

We could only take our medicine and try to put things right again the following year - which is what we did. Stuart left for Newcastle, Bryan Roy went and it felt like we were starting again, similar to when we'd gone down before.

Pierre had come in towards the end of the previous season and some people might say he wasn't a typical Forest signing maybe. But you need that maverick in there at times and he gave us things up top we hadn't really had since Stan left.

Yes, he'd had a bit of a reputation at Celtic, but as long as people fitted into the group in a positive way, they would be accepted. And he was.

Geoff Thomas also came in as a more experienced head and Alan Rogers joined too. 'Tank' was barking mad, never stopped talking, never stopped running. Him and Geoff would run through brick walls for you.

Now, you knew Pierre wasn't going to do that, but you were hoping he would get 20 or 30 goals to get us straight back up.

He and Kev Campbell were unbelievable together - just a fantastic partnership and they tore the First Division to shreds that season. They were both playing a level below where they should have been and they were just frightening together.

After helping Stuart out the previous season, Dave Bassett had taken over as manager officially and he was very strict on how we set up defensively. He spoke a lot about how he wanted us to play and was very clear about things.

We got the ball forward a little bit quicker, but I wouldn't say we were a long ball team.

Dave had that tag from previous clubs, but really it wasn't like that.

We weren't punting long balls, we were playing passes into areas where Kev could run onto things and he was very effective at that. Maybe he'd not been used in the same way elsewhere, but it gave him a new dimension to his game.

Pierre wouldn't be so keen to go into those areas, but he was happy to come short. He wasn't going to be the kind of guy who runs behind defenders because he didn't want to and, truth be told, he wasn't the quickest.

But if you got anything to him around the 18-yard box then you knew we were going to score because he could work his magic.

We sucked teams onto us a little bit, then played a little bit longer where Stoney could run behind, Andy Johnson or Geoff could get in and we'd be through on goal.

It was a great side and we could get at people in more than one way.

I played every league game bar one that season and it was just a fantastic thing to be a part of, again in stark contrast to the year before.

We beat Doncaster 8-0 at their place early on and even though it was the League Cup, results like that still give you confidence.

We were doing really well when we went to Reading in October and I got the chance to re-live my schooldays as a keeper after Dave Beasant got sent off.

We ended up drawing 3-3 but I wasn't to blame for any of the goals - *honestly!*

First off, I had to face the penalty Dave had been sent off for. So no chance there, really. Then there was a free header and the last goal was a one-on-one, so y'know . . . come on lads, *where was the defence?!*

On top of that, I had to borrow Bez's gloves and have you seen the size of his hands? Those things were massive.

On the plus side, I caught a cross, made one save AND got an assist with a long punt upfield that Kev Campbell got on the end of and scored.

Luckily, in a way, that was also the game Stoney missed an open goal that would have put Ronny Rosenthal to shame.

Kev Campbell got clear and squared for him to tap in, but it took a bobble - *allegedly!* - and he spooned it wide. I think it's still on the internet somewhere, unless Steve's had it taken down.

It was so bad, even the Reading fans were singing *'there's only one Steve Stone'*, so it definitely overshadowed my goalkeeping efforts.

Cheers, Stoney!

By April, it was almost a year to the day that we'd gone down and we played Reading at the City Ground with the chance to all-but secure promotion back to the top flight.

It wasn't the prettiest game, but Chris Bart-Williams grabbed a brilliant late winner and the place went absolutely wild.

At the end, the fans piled on the pitch and again it was just great to see the joy other faces after what had gone before.

Pierre had got 34 goals in all competitions and they were literally chairing him around the pitch on their shoulders, so yes, great, great memories of that season.

By the time we went to West Brom for the last game, we were officially Champions and it was a momentous day; about 5,000 Forest fans packed in the away end and just a great atmosphere throughout.

*The singing, the laughs in the dressing room, all just brilliant. A proper Forest celebration.*

For me, it was a mixture of emotions - delighted to be back up and relieved that we'd done it straight away after just one season out.

A few days later we had an open top bus tour and a Civic reception and that was fantastic too. Typical Nottingham weather, a bit overcast, but we had our families on the bus with us and so many people turned out to celebrate, it was just amazing.

You've got to really appreciate these days when they happen, because you know they might not come around too often.

Hearing the fans sing *'There's only one Stevie Chettle'* while carrying the historic Football League trophy was something I'll never forget.

As part of the celebrations, the club arranged for us to have a night out at a teppinyaki restaurant that we used to go to quite a bit.

It was a great night and everyone had a whale of a time, as you can imagine, especially as the club was picking up the bill.

Well, that's what we thought, anyway.

Forest had said they would pay for it - until they saw the drinks bill!

At that point, they said they'd pay for the food - and we got stung for the beer. Well, you can imagine that tab . . !

One hefty whip round later, we'd just about settled up.

But really, we didn't care. Forest were back where they belonged and we were all looking forward to having a right go at the Premier League.

Everything was looking good but even before we kicked a ball, things started to go wrong. Colin Cooper went back to Boro and Kevin Campbell was sold to Trabzonspor. I think that Kev's deal happened while Dave Bassett was still on holiday, so you can probably imagine what he thought about that.

I don't think anyone was delighted with losing two of our best players but if you're unhappy there are ways and means of going about it.

Yes, speak to the manager, speak to the board if you really want - but don't drop your teammates in the brown stuff.

*And, unfortunately, that's what Pierre did.*

At a time when we should have been knuckling down and banding together for a tough season ahead, he just wasn't there.

Whether it's an unwritten rule or not, you just don't do that.

It doesn't get you anywhere, doesn't get the team anywhere and, at the end of it all, you're going to be tarnished with your own brush.

So to say it was frustrating is an understatement.

I was captain by then and eventually Pierre rang me to talk about coming back. I said he'd have to talk to the lads face-to-face to explain what had gone on and apologise.

When the meeting came around, I just sat back, took it all in, and listened to what he said. He'd been promised we'd buy certain players and that hadn't happened.

It's fair to say Geoff had something to say about what Pierre had done, Stoney had something to say about it, but not much was said at the meeting to be fair. What was the point? What was done was done. We couldn't go back and replay the games he'd missed.

His frustrations were justified, but his actions definitely were not. He apologised, to a degree, but then again, he also tried to justify what he did.

That didn't go down well and the message he got from the lads was that it was not the way to go about it.

I understood his frustration, I think we all did. We'd lost two of our best players and, with the best will in the world, we hadn't really replaced them at that point.

We were promised that we would sign better players but it never happened. But there's a way of going about things and just stopping playing isn't it.

You just roll your sleeves up, get on with it and do the best you can for the club.

Obviously, he came back and scored against Derby but ended up virtually celebrating on his own - after a goal against Derby.

*So, I think that told it's own story about the situation.*

What the whole episode did was take away the momentum that we'd built up. When we came up previously, we carried on our winning ways, but with three of our best players gone or missing, it was a real task right from the start that season.

We'd actually started OK, losing narrowly at Arsenal and winning the next two games.

But we didn't win again until virtually New Year's Eve and we were never really out of the bottom three from October onwards. I think things got worse when Dave was sacked and Ron Atkinson came in.

It's fair to say, me and Ron didn't really see eye-to-eye.

In fact, one of the first things he did was drop me and bring Carlton Palmer into the side.

I'm not sure if he didn't like me as player, it certainly looked that way, but he was the manager, so it was fair enough - I had to take it on the chin.

I didn't really understand what Ron was trying to do. For me, it seemed like we went back to how we were under Cloughie at the end, so it was a strange time.

He was from that era and everything was a bit loose in training - lots of five-a-sides that he joined in with as well. I didn't really get it. I thought we'd moved on from that.

He'd done well at some big clubs and had a good career, so he can't have been a bad manager, but he didn't really suit me.

I think the game had probably moved on. But either way, I didn't play too many games under him. He resigned after relegation was confirmed and funnily enough things picked up right at the end as we won our last three games of that season.

But I don't think anyone was fooled and for me, I knew we were at the start of yet another rebuilding process.

When we first went down under Brian Clough, we had the nucleus of a good side and the same again when we went down the season Stuart and Harry had been in charge.

Now, we'd brought some ambitious signings in - Nikola Jerkan and Jean-Claude Darcheville - but they either hadn't been played or hadn't worked out and it was a case of finding new blood and finding our identity again.

I certainly didn't expect to be back in the First Division so quickly and, despite what had happened under Ron Atkinson, I didn't think my time at the club was coming to an end.

Especially when David Platt came in.

I think everyone was really excited by the appointment because he was a really good player and someone I'd been with many years earlier in the England Under-21s so I kind of knew him a bit.

He was very self-driven, which could sometimes come across as rude, when it really wasn't like that.

It was strange because I started off in the team and I think we only lost three of the first dozen or so games.

I didn't realise it at the time, but I got my last Forest goal with a penalty against Walsall in the League Cup.

I'd scored a couple of pens in the Premier League and was chuffed because my uncle always had a pound on me at 50-1 as the first scorer.

So he made a few quid on those days - to make up for all the others when he'd lost out!

Ian Wright had come to us on loan at the start of that season and a couple of games earlier, he'd scored against West Ham and was looking for a hat-trick. Wrighty was my room-mate at the time and was begging me to let him take it even though I was on penalties.

I did and lo and behold, he missed. So when we got that one against Walsall I saw him grab the ball and come running straight over to give it to me to take it. Top man, a lovely touch.

My technique? There wasn't a lot of mind games going on - I just hit it as hard as I could!

We went through that night, but overall I think David wanted to stamp his identity on the football club and the 'old guard' - people like me, Mark Crossley, Ian Woan - didn't last very long under him.

*From someone who was captain the year before, I suddenly found I wasn't involved in a 20-man squad.*

So it was very hard, but when things like that happen, you know your time is up. I had no God-given right to be at Nottingham Forest for the rest of my career, no matter how much I wanted it.

Still, when you've played 500 games for the club and you're told you're not training with the first team now, you're training with the kids . . . that hurts.

But I had to be professional about it and I was.

Me training with the young lads can be uplifting for them and what message would it send out if I come across like some Big Time Charlie who doesn't want to train? I had to be as good, if not better than I'd always been in training to show them the right attitude and the right approach, no matter what else is going on.

Otherwise, they're going to look at me and say: 'Blimey, this guy's played all those games in the first team and his attitude stinks.'

There was no way I'd ever let that happen. I conducted myself professionally and eventually came back into the first team when someone was injured, but by then I knew it was over.

David Platt was quite honest about it with me, saying: 'You don't figure in my plans so if you can find yourself a club, we'll let you go.'

It hurt like hell to hear, but that's life.

What can I say? At least he was straight with me.

Once I'd got over it initially, my first thought was: 'Right, where's Dave Bassett's number?' Harry was now managing Barnsley, so I rang him the following day, filled him in about the situation and we quickly sorted out a month's loan deal. By the time I got to the end of that, we'd arranged an 18-month contract and that was that.

*

I had to move on. It sounds brutal but there was no point sulking or dragging my heels around the place.

There were no sour grapes. I'd loved my time at Forest, loved the club, and given everything I had. But now the manager had told me I wasn't what he wanted and that's football.

I was sad - *really sad* - that I didn't get to say a proper goodbye to the fans, but I think they knew what Forest meant to me. I hope so, anyway.

Up at Barnsley, Geoff Thomas and Neil Shipperley were there, I was in the team every week and we had a good year, better than Forest ironically, getting to the play-off final at Wembley where we just lost out to Ipswich.

However, it was still weird being away from the City Ground.

I joined the club when I was 14 and left when I was 31 so it was a big part of my life. But everything has to evolve and everyone has to move on eventually.

I had two-and-a-half really good years at Barnsley and it's a really good club. After that I moved on to Grimsby and Burton but came back and worked as a coach at Forest for seven years - right from the Under-10s to the Under-23s - so it will always, always, always be a huge part of me.

I was there when Billy Davies was manager and to be honest, I didn't see any progression route to first team coaching, which I was looking for. Maybe if I'd sat on my hands for six months or so, that opportunity may have come up when Stuart Pearce became manager, but that was not to be and I chose a different career path, to go and work in non-league.

The great thing for me is that there are still people who have risen to the first team who I worked with when they were kids, people like Joe Worrall, Matty Cash, Tyler Walker.

If they could go on and do what I did in the Forest shirt, I'd be absolutely delighted for them, because I know how much talent they have and how hard they've worked.

Me? If I had to sum up my career and my time at the club, I'd say that I was privileged.

*It was a privilege to pull on that red shirt every single time and to have made more than 500 appearances for the club that you love, to have won trophies, scored the odd goal, been part of promotion campaigns - it doesn't get any better than that.*

# POWERING AHEAD

Nottingham Forest Powerchair Football Club was formed in partnership with Nottinghamshire Powerchair Football Club and Nottingham Forest Community Trust, the team have been competing at national level since 2011.

It currently competes in the Muscular Dystrophy UK Powerchair Football Championship. The unisex sport enables people with disabilities of all ages, the platform to participate, show off their skills and enjoy the benefits of being in a team.

At the moment the team is getting ready for the new season to begin eager to go for promotion!

## What is Powerchair Football?

Powerchair Football is a unique sport that provides opportunities for people with a high level of impairment to play football. It is the only active team participation sport for people who use electric wheelchairs.

The sport is fast paced, dynamic and enjoyable.

Powerchair Football enables disabled people to take part in regular activity providing them with competition, fun and friendship, as a result it helps build key life skills such as teamwork and communication.

It creates a great social opportunity for the players and their families as they experience the highs and lows of participating in the nation's favourite sport. It brings strangers together, many of whom have similar stories and life experiences, creating friendships and bonds which last a lifetime.

Powerchair football is a unique sport that provides opportunities for people with a high level of impairment to access the game of football. It is the only active team participation sport for people who use electric wheelchairs.

The game is for anyone who uses a powered wheelchair or those who have limited movement in a manual wheelchair. The sport is fast-paced, dynamic and very enjoyable to watch. The unique nature of powerchair football allows all ages, disabilities and both genders to compete together.

Most of all, of course, it's about having fun.

**For further information contact: https://www.facebook.com/Nottingham-Forest-Powerchair-Football-Club-1896502913932977**

# THANK YOU ALL FOR YOUR HELP

Huge thanks to the following, without which this book would not have been possible: Chris Bart-Williams, Ian Woan, David Phillips, Mark Crossley *#walkingsbrilliant*, Jason Lee, Bryan Roy, Nigel Jemson, Des Lyttle, Gary Charles, Steve Chettle, Gary Brazil, Richard Bryans, James Garratt, Andy Livingstone, Craig Armstrong, Charlie Bryans, Natalie Fahy and Marie Wilson at the Nottingham Post, Nottinghamshire.live, Matt Smith, and Ricky Stevenson at Nottingham Forest Powerchair FC, Eva Bart-Williams, Burnley FC, Thomas Telford School, Basford United FC and Lisa Harrison at Bookends.

# PHOTOGRAPHIC CREDITS

All photographs are copyright and courtesy of the *Nottingham Post,* with the exception of the image of Jason Lee and the author *(Page 118)*. Sincere thanks for all your kind and generous help.